FINANCIALLY

Fit

WOMEN

AMANDA THOMPSON

FINANCIALLY
Fit
WOMEN

How to be your own CFO –
Confident, Focused and On top of your money.

First published in 2023 by Dean Publishing
PO Box 119
Mt. Macedon, Victoria, 3441
Australia
deanpublishing.com

DEAN PUBLISHING

Cataloguing-in-Publication Data
National Library of Australia
Title: Financially Fit Women – How to be your own CFO – Confident, Focused and On top of your money.
Edition: 1st edn
ISBN: 978-1-925452-60-0
Category: Business and Finance/Personal Development

*This book is dedicated to three beautiful souls
who have profoundly shaped my life and
touched my heart. Mum, your unwavering
belief in me has always given me wings to soar.
Bella and Livvy, watching you become your
authentic selves fills me with immense pride.
I am grateful for all that you are.*

*To all of the women whom I know or are yet to
meet, this book is also dedicated to you. Know
that I believe in you and that you have the
strength to chase your dreams.*

xxAmanda

CONTENTS

CHAPTER 8: MONEY FOR RETIREMENT
Maximising Your Superannuation and Creating a Retirement Plan

CHAPTER 9: MONEY WHEN YOU SELL YOUR BUSINESS
The Importance of Creating a Small Business Retirement Plan....171

CHAPTER 10: MONEY FOR YOUR FAMILY
Creating a Financial Plan to Provide for Your Loved Ones and Protect Their Future 185

CHAPTER 11: MONEY MASTERY
Achieving Financial Fitness at All Levels of Your Life....................203

BONUS: MY TOP FIVE FINANCIALLY FIT TIPS

"Don't be afraid.
Be focused. Be
determined.
Be hopeful. Be
empowered."

Michelle Obama

FOREWORD
FROM PEACE MITCHELL

Amanda Thompson is one of the most kind-hearted, loyal and generous women I've ever met. When I first met Amanda and heard about her quest to change the world through empowering women to reach their financial potential, my eyes lit up, and my heart sang! Here was someone committed to the same work as us. We believe that investing in women is the most powerful way to change the world. To find someone who shares the same belief, vision and values is rare and exciting.

Amanda is also strong, courageous and fearless. She is an incredible role model to her two beautiful daughters, Livvy and Bella, and as a single mother, she deeply understands the importance of being in control of your finances. Because of this, she is dedicated to elevating women and ensuring that they are equipped with the knowledge and confidence to be proactive in charting the course for their future.

Legacy is a word Amanda often uses when she talks about why she does what she does. Her vision goes far beyond the here and now. It's deeper than this week or this year. Her dream is to create real change for women and for the ripple effects to be felt into the future, benefiting this generation, the next and all those that follow.

As an award-winning financial advisor, you might think that life has been easy for Amanda. But that's not the whole story. She has overcome many obstacles to get to where she is today. Her positive attitude, her endurance to keep going and her determination to stay focused on her goals have seen her come out on top again and again.

I admire Amanda's holistic approach to finance. She encourages people to work out what's important to them and consider all aspects of life, including the dreams they want to achieve. Her approach is ambitious yet realistic, and she has helped many create enduring prosperity that supports their vision for the future.

Financially Fit Women will help you tap into your hidden potential. It will support you to navigate the emotions that are so often tied up with money, helping you to let go of limiting beliefs, fears around scarcity and old money stories. This book will guide you to build your confidence, create a positive relationship with money, establish an optimistic outlook, free yourself from anxiety around your numbers and take charge of your financial future.

Amanda has never let fear stand in her way, and she is a genuine inspiration to others. She believes that we all have the power to choose the direction we take in life. I've seen her utilise this mindset – along with a winning combination of grit and courage – to generate some big wins for herself and others.

Peace Mitchell

Cofounder – The Women's Business School, AusMumpreneur & WCW Press

Chair – Tererai Trent International Foundation

Director – Women Changing the World Investments

Australian Ambassador – WEDO (Women's Entrepreneurship Day Organisation) & Women in Tech Global Movement

WELCOME

I grew up in a single parent family. From an early age, I began to understand the value of money and the notion of having to "budget" to ensure that life ran smoothly. To this day, I appreciate and am in awe of how my mum travelled through the years financially. For those with children who participate in sport – you will be well aware that there is a significant cost involved. My mum somehow managed to financially allow me to compete in any and every sport that I chose, with one condition: that I committed to it.

I remember visiting the career counsellor at school when I was 16, and stating so strongly that I wanted to be an accountant. I loved numbers. I was really good at them. I even took accounting as an "easy" subject, to have a break from the maths and science stream that I had undertaken. I used to challenge myself to see how quickly I could do all of the work, plus my homework, in class. I got so much personal satisfaction from that class. But, my school had other opinions and wanted me to follow the science stream, so accounting was not the degree I completed or the path I took – at least not straight away.

During the majority of my younger years, I was completely addicted to sport. You would have found me following the black line in the swimming pool every morning before school, and most nights after school were spent training for any school team, including netball. As well as finding personal fulfilment in all things numbers, I was also amazed by the human body.

I was told not to pursue an accounting stream at university by my school, they told me to study medicine instead. We compromised with a sports science degree. This goes a long way to explain why I can bring fitness analogies so easily into the finance arena.

It was a twist of fate that took me into the career I have today. A two-week job at a fund manager in the city turned into progressions throughout the industry until I find myself exactly where I am meant to be – writing this book and absorbed by my passion to empower women.

At age 34, I had a heart attack. I was so stressed trying to keep up with work and life and I didn't even know it, until I ended up in intensive care. Four weeks in the hospital and having to slow down forced me to reassess my life and my work. It was during this time that I listened to that inner self and decided to step out of the banking arena and follow my passion to be a financial advisor who challenged the regular ideals.

I often joke when I am running workshops that you shouldn't be like Kaz (Karyn, my mum) – not because of the upbringing I had, but because she didn't understand finances beyond making ends meet and going without to provide for her children. I recall being quite young (in today's terms) and saying to Mum that she should live a bit and not worry so much about paying her home loan down so much. Her response was quite simply, "I don't have much in superannuation, so if anything happens to me, the house is the only asset for you and your brother." How selfless is that? I wish I had known what I do now and been able to guide my mum sooner.

Then it was my turn. I became a single mum at age 33. Lucky for me, at this stage I was a financial advisor and in well-paid employment. I was confident I could survive financially on my own. So (in hindsight, foolishly) I completed a simple financial settlement with my husband that was just a 50/50 agreement across everything. Then the universe had different plans for me, and I got life-threateningly sick and had to leave my well-paid employment to focus on health and being a mum.

In 2016, after moving into boutique practices, and yet still feeling as if something was missing, I decided to embark on my own business. I wanted to build a business that reflected me – that reflected my beliefs and values. But at the time, it seemed like a crazy idea. I was a single mum. I was responsible for keeping a roof over our heads and the cost of raising two young girls. How could I possibly give up a reliable, stable income to launch my own business? The protective woman in me didn't want to jeopardise my children's future. My go-to person, my mum, was concerned I would put myself under too much pressure both financially and personally, because she knows all too well that I give every inch of myself to what I believe in.

But I knew, deep down, that starting my own business was the right decision. The thought of starting my own business just wouldn't go away. So, I listened to my intuition and I came up with a plan. I spent many hours developing a realistic business plan and saving as much as I could to ensure that I had a six-month backup plan. This was to ensure that the girls and I could survive financially. And we did more than survive – we thrived. I now have a portfolio of incredible clients from all walks of life. It has also given me the opportunity to share through this book, with the goal to help as many women as possible.

In the decade I spent as an executive financial advisor at two of the top four banks, I learnt so much more than any textbook could have taught me. I embraced every opportunity to increase my knowledge, both through my professional networks and from the businesses (and the owners) that were my clients. This openness to learn and encounter different scenarios continues to this day. My "style", if you can call it that, is one that encompasses both personal experience and lessons learnt through the years. It is this approach that sets me apart from most of my peers. I see each and every client as a learning opportunity for myself.

I feel gratitude for every Financially Fit Women course I run and every client I mentor, because I get the opportunity to consistently look at my business in the exact way I hope this book assists you to look at yours.

"Invest in yourself.
You can afford
it. Trust me."

Beyonce

HOW TO USE THIS BOOK

To get the most out of this book, it's important to take the time to read each chapter thoroughly and understand each concept fully. The chapters build on each other, so it's crucial to start at the beginning and work your way through to the end.

While some chapters are geared towards women who run businesses, the principles outlined throughout the book can be applied to anyone looking to improve their financial situation. The key to financial fitness, just like with physical fitness, is discipline, consistency and a willingness to push past your comfort zone.

In this book, you'll find knowledge, practical examples and reflection exercises at the end of each chapter. Taking time to reflect allows us to step back, assess our progress, and make any necessary changes to achieve our goals.

With this book, there is an accompanying workbook uniquely designed to help you work through specific financial and personal exercises to help you achieve your goals and fulfil your dreams. This icon will appear when there is an exercise for you to do inside the workbook.

To access the *Financially Fit Women Workbook* that you can use alongside this book, simply go to:

endurancefinancial.com.au/book

WHAT'S INCLUDED

Money Mindset: This chapter covers the pre-work needed to get started, including developing a money mindset, living authentically with your values, understanding your money story, and using money affirmations.

Money Goals: This chapter covers goal-setting for both personal and financial goals, including how to create specific and measurable goals to achieve your desired outcomes.

Money and Business: This chapter gives you an overview of business essentials, such as structure, budget, cashflow and how to create a business plan.

Money for Today: This chapter covers the basics of achieving financial fitness, including understanding cash flow, conducting a spending audit, managing debt, and creating a spending plan.

Money and Wages: This chapter works through the importance of paying yourself a salary and provides an overview of how to achieve this.

Money for the Unexpected: Protection is an essential aspect of financial planning. This chapter covers insurance, including understanding different types, conducting an insurance audit, setting insurance goals, and lessons learnt.

Money for Tomorrow: This chapter covers investing, including different types of investments, conducting an investments audit, setting investment goals, and reflections and lessons.

Money for Retirement: Retirement planning is a crucial aspect of long-term financial planning. This chapter covers superannuation, including understanding superannuation, conducting a superannuation audit, setting retirement goals, and lessons learnt.

Money When You Sell Your Business: This chapter delves into the need to consider your small business retirement plan, including how you plan to receive a financial gain in the long-term.

Money for Your Family: Estate planning is essential for protecting your family's financial future. This chapter covers understanding estate planning, conducting an estate planning audit, setting estate planning goals, and reflections and lessons.

Money Mastery: This chapter covers decision-making, taking action, celebrating successes, and reflections on the financial mastery journey.

Bonus Chapter: My Top Five Financially Fit Tips – Business Edition: This chapter provides additional tips and insights for business owners looking to improve their finances and grow their business.

There is also a financial terminology glossary at the back of the book, to help you with any terms you may not be familiar with. I've also included some hotlines for crisis help and financial support – you can find these at the back of the book and I encourage you to reach out if you ever need.

So, whether you're a business owner or an individual, grab your notebook and pen, and let's get started on the path to financial fitness. Let's create healthy habits that support your long-term goals and enable you to live the life you want.

I'm really excited you're here.

xx Amanda

THE FINE PRINT

Just like stretching before a workout, this needs to come first to get you to your financial best.

I just wanted to take a moment to let you know that the information provided in *Financially Fit Women* is general advice only.

Please keep in mind that just like a personal trainer cannot create a workout plan without knowing your specific fitness level and goals, the strategies and information presented are intended as general advice only and may not be suitable for everyone.

Think about it this way: if you've never run a marathon before, your workout plan will look very different from someone who has completed 10 marathons. That's why I need to remind you that I'm not able to give specific advice to anyone who hasn't engaged my financial planning services.

So, if and when you're looking for personalised financial advice, I strongly encourage you to engage the services of a qualified, independent financial advisor. Look for someone who has deep expertise in your particular area of need – and make sure it's someone who offers personalised advice while making you feel at ease.

Okay, with that out of the way, let's continue!

"The secret of getting ahead is getting started."

Mark Twain

"I've learned that making a "living" is not the same as making a life."

Maya Angelou

CHAPTER 1

MONEY MINDSET

Financial Fitness Starts in the Mind

If I've learnt one thing over my many years in finance, it's that the way you think and feel about your money makes a big difference in how you look after your money.

When I was a guest on *Well, Hello Anxiety*, a podcast hosted by Dr Jodi Richardson, I spoke about money being a huge factor in an anxious mind. I highlighted that one of the most beneficial tools you can have to combat money anxiety is to understand where your money beliefs came from and your fears around money. When I present the questions throughout the following chapters as tasks for my clients, I always give them the choice of sharing with me or not.

The most important person who needs to understand your inner mindset around money is you, and if by completing this task you have some "aha" moments, then you have taken a step in the right direction. In my experience, it is also beneficial to talk through your findings with someone, whether they are a loved one or a financial advisor.

> *Your money mindset is the set of beliefs and attitudes you have towards money, shaped by your experiences and the messages you've received about money throughout your life and your personal values.*

We all know that it's not always easy to see, accept or change our money mindset. Money can be a source of stress and anxiety for many people, and it's easy to fall into negative thought patterns – especially if you're not aware you have them.

But having a positive money mindset means approaching money with a growth mindset, believing that you can improve your financial situation and achieve your goals.

LIVING AUTHENTICALLY

Living authentically and being true to yourself is essential for living a fulfilling and meaningful life. When we embrace who we truly are and align our values with our actions, we experience a sense of purpose and fulfilment that cannot be matched. Too often, we let external factors – like societal expectations or the opinions of others – influence our decisions, leading us to live a life that doesn't reflect our true selves. However, when we make choices that align with our values and beliefs, we experience a deep sense of inner peace and happiness. Living authentically also extends to our finances. When we are influenced by others, we often end up spending money on the things we don't really want or need, to keep up, to fit in and to try and make ourselves feel good. The other problem with money is that it can be hard to talk about. For some people, it can even cause anxiety, lead to arguments and bring on stress. One of the ways we can tackle these issues is by aligning our financial goals with our personal values and beliefs.

Each of us are guided and driven by different things. Who you are, where you have come from and what you have done in your life make you who you are today. This includes your values and your life experiences so far.

VALUES

> Your values are the things that you believe are important
> in the way you live and work. Your values shape the
> decisions you make and the actions you take.

For me, they are a big part of why I stopped working for someone else and started my own business, and how I run my business now. Throughout my years, I have completed many different values exercises. Many of my values became stronger and more apparent as I embraced working for myself.

LIST OF CORE VALUES

ACCEPTANCE	BRILLIANCE	COMPETENCE
ACCOMPLISHMENT	CALM	CONCENTRATION
ACCOUNTABILITY	CANDOUR	CONFIDENCE
ACCURACY	CAPABLE	CONNECTION
ACHIEVEMENT	CAREFUL	CONSCIOUSNESS
ADAPTABILITY	CERTAINTY	CONSISTENCY
ALERTNESS	CHALLENGE	CONTENTMENT
ALTRUISM	CHARITY	CONTRIBUTION
AMBITION	CLEANLINESS	CONTROL
AMUSEMENT	CLEAR	CONVICTION
ASSERTIVENESS	CLEVER	COOPERATION
ATTENTIVE	COMFORT	COURAGE
AWARENESS	COMMITMENT	COURTESY
BALANCE	COMMONSENSE	CREATION
BEAUTY	COMMUNICATION	CREATIVITY
BOLDNESS	COMMUNITY	CREDIBILITY
BRAVERY	COMPASSION	CURIOSITY

DECISIVE	GENIUS	MATURITY
DECISIVENESS	GIVING	MEANING
DEDICATION	GOODNESS	MODERATION
DEPENDABILITY	GRACE	MOTIVATION
DETERMINATION	GRATITUDE	OPENNESS
DEVELOPMENT	GREATNESS	OPTIMISM
DEVOTION	GROWTH	ORDER
DIGNITY	HAPPINESS	ORGANISATION
DISCIPLINE	HARD WORK	ORIGINALITY
DISCOVERY	HARMONY	PASSION
DRIVE	HEALTH	PATIENCE
EFFECTIVENESS	HONESTY	PEACE
EFFICIENCY	HONOUR	PERFORMANCE
EMPATHY	HUMILITY	PERSISTENCE
EMPOWER	IMAGINATION	PLAYFULNESS
ENDURANCE	IMPROVEMENT	POISE
ENERGY	INDEPENDENCE	POTENTIAL
ENJOYMENT	INDIVIDUALITY	POWER
ENTHUSIASM	INNOVATION	PRESENT
EQUALITY	INQUISITIVE	PRODUCTIVITY
ETHICAL	INSIGHTFUL	PROFESSIONALISM
EXCELLENCE	INSPIRING	PROSPERITY
EXPERIENCE	INTEGRITY	PURPOSE
EXPLORATION	INTELLIGENCE	QUALITY
EXPRESSIVE	INTENSITY	REALISTIC
FAIRNESS	INTUITIVE	REASON
FAMILY	IRREVERENT	RECOGNITION
FAMOUS	JOY	RECREATION
FEARLESS	JUSTICE	REFLECTIVE
FEELINGS	KINDNESS	RESPECT
FEROCIOUS	KNOWLEDGE	RESPONSIBILITY
FIDELITY	LAWFUL	RESTRAINT
FOCUS	LEADERSHIP	RESULTS-ORIENTED
FORESIGHT	LEARNING	REVERENCE
FORTITUDE	LIBERTY	RIGOUR
FREEDOM	LOGIC	RISK
FRIENDSHIP	LOVE	SATISFACTION
FUN	LOYALTY	SECURITY
GENEROSITY	MASTERY	SELF-RELIANCE

SELFLESS	STATUS	TRANSPARENT
SENSITIVITY	STEWARDSHIP	TRUST
SERENITY	STRENGTH	TRUSTWORTHY
SERVICE	STRUCTURE	TRUTH
SHARING	SUCCESS	UNDERSTANDING
SIGNIFICANCE	SUPPORT	UNIQUENESS
SILENCE	SURPRISE	UNITY
SIMPLICITY	SUSTAINABILITY	VALOUR
SINCERITY	TALENT	VICTORY
SKILL	TEAMWORK	VIGOUR
SKILLFULNESS	TEMPERANCE	VISION
SMART	THANKFUL	VITALITY
SOLITUDE	TIMELESS	WEALTH
SPIRIT	TOLERANCE	WELCOMING
SPIRITUALITY	TOUGHNESS	WINNING
SPONTANEOUS	TRADITIONAL	WISDOM
STABILITY	TRANQUILITY	WONDER

WHO ARE YOU?

It's easy to lose your identity as you get caught up in life. You might be a mum, an employee or a business owner, a wife, a sister, an aunt, maybe even a volunteer. And it is easy to find yourself feeling lost along the way.

If you wrote a bio that was *truly you*, what would it say?

Think about times when you were most proud of yourself, when you were happiest, and when you felt most fulfilled. With these times in mind, look through the values list above and pick out ten words that really resonate with you. Feel free to add your own words if you can't find the one you are looking for.

Questions to think about:

Now that you've thought about your values, take a moment to stop and reflect. Think about your answers to the following questions.

- What brings you the greatest joy and fulfilment in life?

- What do you feel passionate about, and what drives you to pursue your interests?

- What unique talents and strengths do you possess, and how can you use them to make a positive impact on the world?

- What legacy do you want to leave behind, and how do you want to be remembered?

- What problems or challenges in the world inspire you to take action, and how can you contribute to solving them?

- What kind of impact do you want to have on the people around you, and how can you use your skills and resources to make a difference in their lives?

- What motivates you to get up every day, and what kind of life do you want to create for yourself and those you care about?

The workbook provides some further exercises to work through your Values and Living Authentically.

YOUR MONEY STORY

Money is often a subject that people worry about, and who can blame them?

Money and finances can be tricky, demoralising and completely frustrating. No one wants to be destitute, hungry, or lacking resources. We all know that money is important – both understanding it and talking about it.

So why do we have such a hard time talking about it? Whether you've fallen on hard financial times, feel unable to accomplish your money goals, or struggle with financial literacy, it is because it is such an emotionally charged subject, and with that emotion comes fear. But you are used to hard things. So, just because 'money' is hard, it doesn't mean we get to avoid it.

> *I am a firm believer that every single financial decision we make is backed by an emotion.*

It's important to think about our emotions while making financial decisions, and explore why you're making these decisions. Working on awareness will empower you to make the best financial decisions. That way, you can feel confident to take positive actions to further improve your financial life. Remember, the hardest part about creating any habit is starting it. If we can realise that talking about money isn't about our understanding of spreadsheets, maths problems or even our tax returns – and that it is actually talking about our feelings – then we are on the right path to starting.

Your money story is the foundation of your financial fitness journey, providing invaluable insight into your relationship with money. It's like warming up before a race – essential for achieving your performance goals. By exploring your past experiences and memories around money, you can identify patterns and behaviours that may be holding you back from achieving financial success. But don't worry, if you find this process difficult, you're not alone. Just like how athletes often feel nervous before a race, financial anxiety is a common challenge.

By embracing your money story and understanding your relationship with money, you'll be able to make positive changes and achieve greater financial fitness. Here are some questions designed for you to take a deep look into your past and begin to understand where and why each of your 'money beliefs' developed.

Questions to think about:

• Do you avoid talking about money? If so, why?

• Write three sentences to describe how you feel about money. Example: Budgeting scares me.

• Tell the story of your first recollection of money.

- Recall a childhood experience that related to the value of money.

- What is your first money memory directly related to being a business owner?

- Are there any other standout money memories for you?

- What is one money tragedy you have personally experienced?

- What is one money triumph you have personally experienced?

- Describe your current money situation.

- How are you responsible for this situation?

- How do you gauge your money? Do you spend or save?

- What does being financially comfortable look like to you?

 You will find a Money Story exercise in the workbook.

Tips for your money mindset

1. Know you are not alone.
One thing that is important to me is to get people sharing and talking. I can guarantee there isn't much I haven't seen or heard in my business, so I can safely tell you that you are not alone. So, don't be afraid to share the burden you are feeling. There should be no such thing as financial shame.

2. Take time out.
Like anything else that stresses us, if we stay in the moment with our heads spinning around and around, there is every chance we will find ourselves delving deeper into stress. Walk away and take time out. Come back to thinking about it with a clear head.

3. Ask for help.
Our anxiety increases when we feel we will never overcome a challenge. Asking for support lessens the burden on us as individuals by creating collaboration and community, and makes tasks feel more achievable.

4. Avoid worst-case thinking.
Remember, just because we aren't great at one thing doesn't mean we are a failure at life. Keep things in perspective.

5. Create a positive habit.
Feel those endorphins multiply. And don't forget to celebrate your successes!

"Rather than focusing on the obstacle in your path, focus on the bridge over the obstacle."

Mary Lou Retton

MONEY AFFIRMATIONS

A lot of people have a negative relationship with money and their future financial security. They may believe that they may lose everything they have (such as their job that pays well) or that they won't have enough money to have a financially secure retirement. When we break the cycle of negative thoughts, we can also break the limiting beliefs we have and increase our money confidence.

The basic idea of affirmations is that they are powerful, positive thoughts that you repeat to yourself over and over again until they become a reality. As we know, the fear and negativity around money can be cumbersome and disheartening. Affirmations around money are ones that are specifically designed to help you change your thoughts about money, and open your mind to think more positively about it.

Here are some affirmations to use as tools to shape your money reality.

I deserve to have all that I need

I am open to receiving abundance

I am creating wealth

My relationship with money is healthy

Money is a positive tool in my life

I can turn my skills into profit

Money is not an end, but a means to
achieve what is important to me

I trust my judgement to make good
financial decisions

I am wealthy beyond money

I am smart with my money

It makes me happy to spend responsibly

I release all resistance to attracting money

I am worthy of positive cashflow

I deserve to be paid for my skills,
knowledge and hard work

I can look at my finances without fear

> *At the end of the day, I want you to truly*
> *believe that you have the power to create the*
> *success and build the wealth you desire.*

Take some time to write down your own money affirmations that counteract the negative beliefs you uncovered in the previous lesson. For example, if you identified a negative belief that you don't deserve to be wealthy, you can write an affirmation such as "I am deserving of wealth and abundance in my life."

When writing your affirmations, make sure to use positive language and focus on what you want to attract into your life, rather than what you want to avoid. For example, instead of saying "I don't want to be in debt," you can say "I am debt-free and financially secure."

Once you have written your affirmations, repeat them to yourself regularly, ideally every day. You can say them out loud, write them down, or even create visual reminders, such as sticky notes or screensavers on your phone or computer.

Remember, just like with physical exercise, consistency is key when it comes to practicing money affirmations. With dedication and effort, you can shift your mindset towards positivity and abundance, and start attracting more financial success and security into your life.

REFLECTIONS AND LESSONS

Great job on finishing this chapter!

How did you find working through these questions? Believe it or not, I find delving into who I am and then consequently talking about it all quite difficult. You may also feel the same. As with all areas of this book that give you some angst, please remember to be kind to yourself. This isn't a "leave pass" to not complete this chapter, but permission to give yourself some space. Walk away for a bit if you need to and then come back to it. I promise you, whatever I ask you to do throughout the book, I have completed myself, and I've seen it help others to become financially empowered.

Remember, defining your personal values is an ongoing process, and it's okay to refine and adjust them over time as you grow and evolve. I encourage you to return to your values multiple times throughout the book.

By living in alignment with your personal values, you can create a fulfilling and authentic life financially (and otherwise) that reflects who you truly are.

(1) > (2) > (3) > (4) > (5)

Remember   Understand   Analyse   Apply   Extend

1. REMEMBER:

What were some of the specific skills, knowledge, or habits that you gained during this chapter?

2. UNDERSTAND:

Why are these accomplishments important for your financial fitness? How will they impact your life in the short-term and long-term?

3. ANALYSE:

What were some of the positive/helpful behaviours you've noticed you have? And what were some of the negative/unhelpful behaviours that you need to be aware of going forward?

REFLECTIONS & ACTIONS
4. APPLY:

Where and how can you apply the knowledge and skills you gained during this chapter? What are some of the specific areas where you can apply your new financial literacy, and how will you do so?

....

....

....

....

....

....

....

....

....

....

....

....

....

5. EXTEND:

How can you use the knowledge and skills you gained during this chapter in other parts of your life? How can you extend the benefits of financial fitness beyond just your personal finances?

Just as rest and recovery are critical components of physical fitness, reflection plays a vital role in becoming financially fit.

It allows us to pause, take a step back, and evaluate our progress towards our goals.

Without reflection, we risk falling into old habits and repeating the same mistakes.

By reflecting on our actions and decisions, we can gain insight into what works for us and what doesn't, and make the necessary adjustments to achieve success.

So just as we make time for stretching and warm-ups in our physical fitness routine, we must also prioritise regular reflection to keep our minds and actions aligned with our goals.

"Vulnerability is the birthplace of innovation, creativity and change."

Brené Brown

"Money is like a sixth sense – and you can't make use of the other five without it."

Mae West

CHAPTER 2

MONEY GOALS

Setting and Achieving
Your Financial Objectives

PERSONAL GOALS

While we know that money can provide us with financial security, it does not always correspond to personal wellbeing or living a fulfilling life.

> *Our dreams and our goals are what drive us forward and give us direction.*

You might have business dreams and goals, or personal ones, or it's possible they are both intertwined together. These goals will drive everything you do in life, including in your business, so it's important to have them clearly thought-out.

Now that you've had time to reflect on yourself through money mindset, it's time to set new goals and work towards achieving them.

Just like in fitness, setting goals is essential to achieving success. Without clear goals, it's easy to get off track and lose motivation.

Take a moment to set your goals. Create short-, medium- and long-term goals using the following outline.

Write down your dreams and goals – you can use the goal setting sheet in the workbook as your guide. After you write your goals, start brainstorming about what you need to do to achieve these goals.

Write down at least 15 personal goals. They do not need to be money-orientated at all; see the following examples.

Example: Take my family out to dinner once a month.

Example: Get a massage every fortnight.

Prioritise your top five "right now" goals.

Are you ready to set your personal goals? Research shows those who write down their goals are more likely to achieve them. Head to the workbook and let's get started.

STOP. KEEP. START.

The 'Stop. Keep. Start.' process extends on the goals you have set and assists you to delve further into how you are going to achieve them. As the name suggests, you are identifying the habits or actions that you need to **stop** doing, **keep** doing and **start** doing in order to set the path to achieving your goals.

STOP
What is counterproductive to my purpose and values? What are the actions, beliefs, or attitudes that **stop** or hold you back from achieving your goals?

KEEP
Identify the things that are working well that you want to **keep** or that align with your purpose and values that are contributing to moving you forward to success.

START

What do you need to **start** doing in order to achieve your goals? Begin with taking a deep breath, and take the steps towards your goals and success.

1. Write each separate goal and its corresponding dollar figure down on the top line.

2. Make a list of all the tasks you need to stop, keep and start to achieve this goal.

Record your Stop Keep Start intentions in the workbook.

FINANCIAL GOALS

Money goals are specific financial targets that we set ourselves. These goals may include savings targets, investments, debt reduction or passive income. They are important to create as they use your values to make financial choices that align with your beliefs, create meaningful goals, and develop healthy habits.

Before you get started, take a moment to consider your personal definition of success. What does success mean to you now that you know your money story and you have started using money affirmations?

Now that you have identified your personal values and goals, take some time to explore how you can integrate them into who you want to be financially.

> *Two of the major benefits of setting money goals are financial security and accountability.*

As you have discovered, the majority of our personal goals align with our long-term vision of the life we want to live. However, while on the surface they are not money specific, there is often a money value attached to them that allows us to achieve our long-term security.

Money goals and the processes we set out to achieve them also provide a sense of accountability, in order to track our progress to success. Committing to and then owning our financial decisions creates one of the greatest feelings of achievement and empowerment.

EXAMPLES OF FINANCIAL GOALS
Income goals
Income goals often include salary increase targets, promotion within your current employment or even entrepreneurship. In the following chapter, you will learn that income goals are not made as part of cashflow planning.

Savings goals

Savings goals include saving a set sum of funds to purchase an asset (such as a deposit on a house), provide for set expenses (such as schooling) or even an event (such as a wedding or a holiday). I wonder if you consider savings goals to include an "emergency" or "peace of mind" sum.

Investment Goals

Investment goals generally relate to long-term financial plans and can include avenues of passive income or event retirement planning.

Debt-reduction Goals

Debt-reduction goals relate to specific reduction of debt such as credit card, tax debt or home mortgage.

Money goals can be short- or long-term, but they must be both specific and measurable. For example, your goal might be: I need to save $30,000 capital to start a business in 2 years. They also need to be reasonable and achievable, which encourages us to monitor our progress; otherwise, we will lose confidence in our ability to achieve them and likely give up on them.

Questions to think about:

- What does financial freedom mean to you?

- What role do financial resources play in achieving your personal values and life goals?

- How do your financial decisions reflect your personal values?

- Even if you had unlimited funds, what would you still not ever buy?

- How do your financial goals align with your personal values and long-term aspirations?

- What steps can you take to ensure your financial decisions align with your personal values and contribute to a more meaningful and fulfilling life?

You can dive deeper into your own money goals in the workbook.

A QUICK WORD ON BUSINESS GOALS

Make sure to align your business practices with your values and manage your finances in a way that is consistent with your values. If not, you may lose motivation during the challenging aspects of running a business. Always check if your decisions are in line with your values, and this will simplify things and allow you to enjoy your work.

Questions to think about:

- What do you want to be able to say about your business in one year?

- What are you loving about your business?

- What are the top three things you are focusing on this year?

- What gives you sleepless nights in regard to your business?

REFLECTIONS AND LESSONS

Another chapter complete!

It's important to have both personal and money goals. By going through the process of setting and analysing your goals, you gain clarity on the actions you need to take in order to set you on the path to achieving them.

> *By setting personal goals, we can evaluate what truly matters to us individually and what will bring us joy and purpose. By setting and working towards our money goals, we support our personal goals by providing resources to achieve the life we want to live.*

Remember, setting goals and creating the plan to achieve them is only a small part of the process. Being accountable for your actions and making adjustments as required will lead you to achieving your goals. It is important to remember that goal setting is an ongoing process and you should revisit these as you make progress towards achieving those that you have set out during this chapter.

① > ② > ③ > ④ > ⑤

Remember　　Understand　　Analyse　　Apply　　**Extend**

1. REMEMBER:

What were some of the specific skills, knowledge, or habits that you gained during this chapter?

2. UNDERSTAND:

Why are these accomplishments important for your financial fitness? How will they impact your life in the short-term and long-term?

3. ANALYSE:

What were some of the positive/helpful behaviours you've noticed you have? And what were some of the negative/unhelpful behaviours that you need to be aware of going forward?

REFLECTIONS & ACTIONS
4. APPLY:

Where and how can you apply the knowledge and skills you gained during this chapter? What are some of the specific areas where you can apply your new financial literacy, and how will you do so?

5. EXTEND:

How can you use the knowledge and skills you gained during this chapter in other parts of your life? How can you extend the benefits of financial fitness beyond just your personal finances?

Just as rest and recovery are critical components of physical fitness, reflection plays a vital role in becoming financially fit.

It allows us to pause, take a step back, and evaluate our progress towards our goals.

Without reflection, we risk falling into old habits and repeating the same mistakes.

By reflecting on our actions and decisions, we can gain insight into what works for us and what doesn't, and make the necessary adjustments to achieve success.

So just as we make time for stretching and warm-ups in our physical fitness routine, we must also prioritise regular reflection to keep our minds and actions aligned with our goals.

"Your time is
limited, don't
waste it living
someone
else's life."

Steve Jobs

CHAPTER 3

MONEY AND BUSINESS

Building Strong
Financial Foundations
for Entrepreneurial Success

UNDERSTANDING BUSINESS
The difference between a hobby and a small business

A hobby is an activity that you do in your spare time for recreation, usually because you enjoy it. A business is a structured, planned activity that hopefully allows for an income after expenses are paid.

No matter what your hobby is, the difference between a hobby and a business has nothing to do with how much money you earn. In fact, many hobbies have a financial outlay, and it is possible to spend more than you actually earn.

> *I want you to know that you are allowed to make money from your passion. Working for yourself and doing what you love means you choose your own hours, breaks and holidays. You have an opportunity to set up a system that works around your lifestyle, family and interests.*

Take a moment to think about your business.
- Is it done with the intention of making a profit?
- Are you going to be running it like a business?
- Do you plan on doing these activities regularly and consistently with a long-term commitment?

BUSINESS STRUCTURES AND OTHER ESSENTIALS

There is a lot to consider when it comes to how to set up your business and all the bits involved. There are some big differences in the types of business structures available and the pros and cons for your business, so it's important to think about what suits you most.

BUSINESS STRUCTURE

> It's important to get the structure of your business right. This is where having a good accountant, tax advisor, financial advisor, someone with all of those skills, or a team of people with those skills will be really useful.

There are a number of different business structures. The simplest is a sole trader. The next step up from that is partnerships. If you're going into business with someone, a partnership is a very simple structure. Then the other options are a family trust or a company. Regardless of what you choose, all businesses should be registered with the relevant regulatory bodies.

SOLE TRADER

A sole trader is a business owned and operated by a single person. The owner is liable for the business debts and obligations.

PARTNERSHIP

A partnership is a business owned and operated by a two or more people. Each partner is liable for the business debts and obligations.

TRUST

A trust is a legal structure where a trustee holds the assets of the business and manages the business, on behalf of and for the benefit of beneficiaries. The main benefit of a trust is that it holds assets separately from the individual and therefore provides asset protection.

COMPANY

A company is a separate legal entity owned by shareholders. A company structure provides protection to the personal assets of the shareholders as there is limited liability for the debts and obligations. Companies are subject to more regulations than other structures such as sole traders and partnerships.

They are the more common business structures in small businesses. When deciding on the most appropriate structure for your business, consider liability, taxation and compliance. There are pros and cons of each, so it's important to have the right advice and knowledge about what suits your situation best.

These business structures offer different degrees of flexibility when it comes to allowing people to join or exit the business. Flexibility around the allocation of income should also be factored into your decision.

When setting up a business, one of the things you need to look at is how the business is going to be funded; it might be some time before the business can fund itself. You might be looking to put cash into the business in order to get it started. Is that cash going to draw on your own resources and savings, or is it money that you need to borrow and put into the business?

If you're funding the business in your own right and loaning the money to the business, there are tax consequences for putting the money in and taking it out. Again, it's important to get these processes in line to make sure this is set up well.

Once you've laid the foundation, got the right team around you, including the right advisors, and you've got the right structure, you're ready to go.

There are a whole lot of potential ongoing issues that you're going to need to be aware of, so having the right people around you is essential to help consider and mitigate any issues.

> *Successful people surround themselves with successful people who they can trust and rely on.*

Depending on the size of your business, these successful people might actually work within your business or might be external to your business, in consulting or specialist roles. There might be people you don't work with more than once a year, but make sure you have those people there to bring the skillsets that you're going to need in your business.

FINANCIAL TERMINOLOGY

As you begin your personal wealth journey or start your business, you will encounter numerous financial terms and acronyms. Although these new terms can be daunting, it's not necessary to feel overwhelmed. To assist you, I have included a glossary section containing definitions of many common financial terms you may come across at the back of the book.

BUSINESS REFLECTION

> *We often make lots of assumptions about our business, but rarely stop to reflect on the data or what's really going on.*

When you are actually reviewing your business and the successes of a business, it takes time because you're going through and figuring out what benefits you get from your business. The easiest way to do that is to think about what benefits you would be getting if you worked for someone else – would you get a phone, a laptop, a car allowance or a fuel allowance? That expense back in your own hand is something that you've actually taken from your business, so you can start to enjoy the success of your business.

Do this as surface-level or as in-depth as you need. However you do it, you need to really go through your expenses. This means getting your financials (including personal or business bank statements) out and taking the time to look through and appreciate what your business is actually giving you in a financial sense. It's not something we do very often, and therefore we don't celebrate what we're getting from our business – so let's start.

It's easy to make assumptions, but to really understand how profitable your business is, you need to dig into the numbers. You can use your accounting software reports where possible, but don't take the easy path. If they don't list this out in a way that fits the software or templates, you will need to spend some time doing this manually.

LET'S TALK NUMBERS

I think we can all agree that our business finances are one of the most intimidating parts of running a business. My clients often share that their biggest fear is that a bad financial decision could be disastrous for the business.

So, why are our finances so often put in the 'too hard' basket? Is it because we are scared of what we don't know, or because we worry that we'll lose our credibility as business owners if we don't understand it all?

Many business owners focus on what they are passionate about and will usually skip over the big picture. They are either too busy or don't have the inclination or the education to understand what the numbers mean.

Remember, sound business decisions are made when we consider our financial goals and understand how the decision will affect the business in the short-term and long-term. When you understand what the financial side of your business looks like, you can develop an understanding of trends, form insights, and make smart decisions – instead of feeling like you're having a stab in the dark.

What is the 'right' way when it comes to our business dollars? Like most things, financial literacy can be developed – with practice. I'm happy to show you the 'right' way to make sense of your business dollars.

I've provided a template in the workbook that you can fill out to review your business.

PROFIT

Profit is the monetary "gain resulting from the employment of capital in any transaction", gross profit is "gross receipts less the immediate costs of production" and net profit is the "amount remaining after deducting all costs from gross receipts".[1] In the simplest terms, profit is the money that remains (in theory) from all of your hard work and revenue generation, once all expenses (including tax) have been paid.

Often, profit is described as the bottom line. The reason it's called the bottom line is because it's the very last line of your financials, that sits at the bottom of financial statements. It is the key figure when you account for everything. What I want you to think about is that if you're investing in a blue-chip company, the goal of that company is to make money for its shareholders. In your small business, you're the shareholder – so why shouldn't you be working to get money out of your business too?

Profit is by far the most-used metric for determining the success of a business. I want to delve deeper into that, because if you are the shareholder, the success of your business directly relates to your personal financial growth.

YOUR BUSINESS' PROFITS

I want you to ask yourself, does your business make a regular profit? Do you *know* if your business makes a regular profit? I want you to feel comfortable about this and I want to empower you to start making the tiniest of changes for the better, starting today.

Here's the more important question – did your business bank account increase by the same amount as your net profit? Now, what I mean by 'net profit' is what's yours after your pay cheque. If you've got a profit that you owe tax on, is there sufficient money in the bank account to pay it?

WHAT TO DO WITH YOUR PROFIT

What do you do with your profit if you do make one? Do you take it out of the business? Do you put it back into the business? Do you have no idea what to do with it? Have you already spent it and it's just a figure on a line?

If you are a sole trader, my question to you is: is your profit that's shown on your tax return greater than your living costs? Is there money sitting there at the end of the day? If you're taking some of your profit, are you taking it as dividends? Or are you paying yourself a salary?

FINANCIAL STATEMENTS, TRUE PROFITS AND YOUR BUSINESS' SUCCESS

Financial statements for small businesses are indeed a true reflection of the success of your business. So, what we need to do is go one step further and understand what the true profit of your business is and where, most importantly, this profit benefits you. It doesn't matter what the company is; every single expense needs to be absolutely perfect and true for that profit to be true. Every single expense in the business needs to be 100% for the business.

"In the future, there will be no female leaders. There will just be leaders."

Sheryl Sandberg

MISTAKES YOU MIGHT BE MAKING

So many sources will quote that the underlying reasons for small businesses not surviving are mostly financial. The good news is that I promise you don't need a finance degree to grow a financially successful business.

Over the last two decades (please don't calculate my age), I have worked with businesses across many different industries and of all sizes. Two of the most common mistakes I see small business owners making are:

1. **Lack of cashflow planning:** cashflow planning is essentially ensuring there is enough money coming in each month and a controlled amount going out. It considers all expected revenue and expenses (including wages, superannuation and taxes).

2. **Lack of personal financial planning:** often, as small business owners, we subscribe to the 'build it, and they will come' method and are fuelled by our passion. We forget that our tank also needs some financial input. What are your long-term personal financial goals, and how is your business going to assist you in achieving them?

Have I managed to hit one of your pain points? When it comes to your numbers, "failing to plan is planning to fail" rings true. The numbers are important because they tell you the story of your business through the past, present, and future.

Don't despair – you don't need to be an accountant. However, knowing the numbers is essential to working smarter in your business. So, here are my top three numbers you should be paying attention to.

THREE NUMBERS TO PAY ATTENTION TO IN YOUR BUSINESS

In my own business, these are the three numbers I look at on a weekly basis to see how my business is tracking.

1. Bank balance

Don't mistake profit for cash. Cashflow is an important metric that keeps all businesses operational. Compared to the budget, you will have real-time insights into how your business is truly tracking and can make business decisions confidently.

While it may be beneficial to budget your revenue and expenses, cashflow planning is where the money is. A well-prepared cashflow budget will allow you the foresight of when the speed bumps may be coming. This is especially important for seasonal businesses.

2. Turnover/revenue generated

This is the total amount of money that comes into the business and comes from all income streams. Take the time to review your revenue and revenue streams and how they are tracking compared to your budget. It is also important to understand why these things are happening. This is where you become proactive with your financial future.

If revenue is lower than budget, you can make decisions immediately and decide how to rectify this in the coming months, instead of turning a blind eye. Conversely, if revenue is higher than budget, it may present an opportunity for further growth.

3. Owner's wages

Last but perhaps most importantly is how much you actually pay yourself. When it comes to paying themselves from their business income, an unfortunate majority of small business owners forgo a wage or salary, preferring to simply take what they need from the business. The reasons for this can include fear of draining the business funds or a lack of understanding of the best way to remunerate themselves.

When you don't pay yourself, you are delaying your personal financial future. Paying yourself should not be a reward; it should be a requirement that you meet regularly. It is also a measure of the health of your business.

If this sounds like gobbledygook to you, don't panic and read on!

BUSINESS CASHFLOW

Most people budget based on what they are going to earn (the money that comes in and how they are going to spend it), but I like to challenge that way of thinking.

> *I believe that to have a useful budget that can also be used for accurate tracking, you have to have knowledge and expectations of your cashflow.*

The key to anything from here on in is really having accurate data. I know, this takes time, but I am going to give a little plug to a good accounting software system which makes adjustments so much easier – hint hint: Xero.

This is where you really need your chart of accounts set up properly. To truly gauge the monetary success of your business for yourself, you need to be able to easily view where the money is coming from and where it is going.

Cashflow forecasts are the beneficial way to protect yourself from 'speed bumps' (or even ditches) throughout the year. If you can clearly see when and where the pressure is going to hit, you can prepare for a buffer. Forecasts provide an opportunity to assess the effects and timing of different options. Cashflow forecasting can help you produce budgets.

If any of the end-of-month lines are in the red, we need to figure out how to deal with that now, before it occurs.

The first thing is to check your expenses. Can you immediately see where you can bring some down to allow more cash in the business, either to spend on generating revenue or to send to yourself in the long run?

Remember the overarching purpose of this book is to provide you with the tools and education to pay yourself what you are truly worth.

YOUR BUSINESS PLAN

A good (and useful) business plan outlines your strategy for the upcoming year. You'll find these can often be used as supporting commentary for grants or bank lending – but it is most important for you to use as your roadmap for the growth and success of your business.

My suggestion is to keep your plan as short as possible. Stick to the key points that you can come to at any time to realign or motivate yourself with.

KEY TIPS FOR CREATING A BUSINESS PLAN YOU ACTUALLY USE:
- Make it professional; take the time to do this.
- Be realistic.
- Remember your target clients.
- Include your pricing model.
- Include Stop, Keep, Start.
- Include your cash forecasts.

Your business vision

Note that when creating goals for your business, they don't have to be monetary goals (I believe this comes naturally), but they can be if that is how you measure your business success.

I caution making a statement on profit though, for the reasons I have mentioned and will expand upon throughout this book.

Example: To have 50 women go through the Financially Fit Women course.

Example: To double my turnover.

Business timeline

Think about your business timeline.

- Where is the business now? Consider all elements of your business, such as your offering, turnover, staff, and available resources.
- Where will the business be in six months? List specific targets that will help you achieve your vision.
- Where will the business be in 12 months? List specific targets that will help you achieve your vision.

HOW WILL YOU GET THERE?

Once you know where you want to go, you need a clear plan for how you want to get there.

Think about the strategies that might work for your business. Areas of consideration can include: personal development, recruiting plan, process improvement, cashflow considerations, increasing customer base.

THINK ABOUT:
- Strategy
- Action Plan (how)
- Timing (completion date)
- Person Responsible

ONE-PAGE ACTION PLAN

Keep in mind your target market and your business goals, and consider what strategies you want to use to make that happen.

If you already have a business plan, take some time to review it and make sure it is still current.

A one-page plan is a simple tool where you can set goals for your business and note down actions you will need to take in your business to achieve these goals. The example in the workbook is the most basic business plan – you can build on it however you want.

When you have completed this action plan, make sure it is somewhere that's easy to refer to, so that your goals and actions are always front of mind.

Fill out your personal action plan in the template provided for you in the workbook.

REFLECTIONS AND LESSONS

A business doesn't just generate income – it can also build your wealth. If you're going down that path, you might have another strategy on the side that enables you to build even more, so the business can generate an income and the income comes out of the business and into another wealth-building strategy.

Depending on the type of business, you might have a few strategies that work hand-in-hand. It's important to work with a financial professional who can help guide you through those decisions.

① ❯ ② ❯ ③ ❯ ④ ❯ ⑤
Remember   Understand   Analyse   Apply   Extend

1. REMEMBER:

What were some of the specific skills, knowledge, or habits that you gained during this chapter?

....

....

....

....

....

....

2. UNDERSTAND:

Why are these accomplishments important for your financial fitness? How will they impact your life in the short-term and long-term?

3. ANALYSE:

What were some of the positive/helpful behaviours you've noticed you have? And what were some of the negative/unhelpful behaviours that you need to be aware of going forward?

REFLECTIONS & ACTIONS
4. APPLY:

Where and how can you apply the knowledge and skills you gained during this chapter? What are some of the specific areas where you can apply your new financial literacy, and how will you do so?

5. EXTEND:

How can you use the knowledge and skills you gained during this chapter in other parts of your life? How can you extend the benefits of financial fitness beyond just your personal finances?

Just as rest and recovery are critical components of physical fitness, reflection plays a vital role in becoming financially fit.

It allows us to pause, take a step back, and evaluate our progress towards our goals.

Without reflection, we risk falling into old habits and repeating the same mistakes.

By reflecting on our actions and decisions, we can gain insight into what works for us and what doesn't, and make the necessary adjustments to achieve success.

So just as we make time for stretching and warm-ups in our physical fitness routine, we must also prioritise regular reflection to keep our minds and actions aligned with our goals.

"I define myself.
I create my
own destiny."

Dr Tererai Trent

CHAPTER 4

MONEY FOR TODAY

Strategies for Achieving Financial Stability

Think about your current approach to your finances. So much of our anxiety about money comes from the unknown – not knowing where our money is going, not having a plan for our money, or not having a plan should our income decline or cease altogether. Do you, or have you ever, lived from payday to payday? I am sure that most people reading this will be nodding.

In this chapter, we are going to get a grasp on the current state of play. If you can develop a sound understanding of your personal financials, you will be able to plan your cashflow and meet your goals.

It's very easy to make assumptions about where our money is going, whether we have enough money to cover our monthly expenses, enough insurance if something were to go wrong, or enough money to go on an annual holiday.

> *The fact is, most people don't really know exactly where their money is going. It's time to change that!*

But first, let us work through that dreaded "b" word. Yes, I mean "budget." Just like the word "diet", budget has such negative connotations. It feels so restrictive, prescriptive and rigid. When we think of the word "budget", we think about penny pinching, sacrificing enjoyment for financial stability and living within limited means. Depending on our own money story, this may be very triggering.

It is far more practical to set a forecast or spending plan, and adjust it as often as necessary to suit the needs of you as an individual.

> *Every single person has their own money story, goals and needs, and a one-size-fits-all approach should never be applied.*

Money and feelings are inseparable. Budgets are designed to help you meet financial goals. However, the problem is that often, if you are told you must restrict yourself in any sense, the task automatically becomes laborious and feels like a chore.

If we instead tell ourselves that we have a spending plan, we no longer feel restricted or inhibited in our ability to make our money work for us. We will feel confident and empowered to take positive action to improve our financial position.

> *By reframing the way we think about "spending plans" (budgets), we can start to see them as positive tools for achieving our financial goals and living a more intentional life.*

SPENDING AUDIT

In any given month, how do you spend your money, what do you do with any surplus, and how are you building wealth? Starting the process of a spending audit can feel completely overwhelming as money is a very emotive subject for so many people, and the greatest emotion attached is usually fear.

So many people have a negative relationship with money and are genuinely fearful for their future financial security. They often believe that there is a high likelihood that they may lose everything (eg. their job that pays well) or that they won't have enough money to have a financially secure retirement. When we break the cycle of negative thoughts, we can also break the limiting beliefs we have and increase our money confidence.

Let's get started by collecting our spending data. Remember that we are trying to identify gaps and areas for improvement so we can empower ourselves – so be kind to yourself.

Documents to gather:
- Last three months of bank statements
- Last three months of credit card statements

Things to consider:
- Start to break down your spending into categories, including essential living (mortgage, rent, groceries, insurance, vehicle etc.) and lifestyle expenses (gym memberships, subscription services, entertainment, travel etc.).

- Compare these expenses to your monthly income.
- Calculate the surplus or deficit you have left at the end of each month.

Figure out if you have a surplus or a deficit in your cashflow. Use this knowledge to make decisions for your life and family. Use this to reshape and inform your goals. In the following chapters, I'll be talking about investment strategies and giving you some amazing insight into how to build wealth, using the cash surplus you create by building a spending plan.

Please note: If this task has uncovered a significant deficit, given you an awareness of a critical debt situation or increased your anxiety, please seek further assistance from a qualified financial counsellor or financial advisor.

You will find a list of organisations that provide free services at the back of this book.

Fill out your spending plan in the template provided for you in the workbook.

DEALING WITH DEBT

Debt is not inherently bad. However, we do need to make allowances for it in your spending plan and forecast. Building your debt management into your spending plan will enable you to feel more in control and have a plan as to when you will be able to pay it off. You will be amazed at what an impact having a plan to pay off debt will have on your mindset.

Most of us will have had experience with debt, whether it is a home loan, a car loan, a credit card or education debt. You need a clear plan for repayment and also a backup plan, in case of the unexpected. As a part of this plan, you also need to gauge what debt is tax-deductible (eg. investment lending) as opposed to non-deductible (eg. your own home).

Continually refinancing your credit cards to a new "interest-free" offer is not the solution to overall debt reduction.

Here is my list of tips to reducing your debt:

Know your debts

Make a list of exactly how much you owe to each provider, what the repayment terms are (date due and minimum amount due) and (the yuck part) the interest cost to you. While this will often be an uncomfortable exercise, sometimes it is just the wakeup call you need to commit to repaying these as quickly as possible.

Prioritise

Work out which debts are high priority to pay off (bad debt and high interest rate first).

Budget

Compare what you earn to what you spend. We all know which way the surplus should fall!

Consolidate

Often, having one repayment is easier to control. Warning: too often, I see people buy cars with the equity in their home to enjoy the lower interest rate. Remember the life span of a car – it is definitely not 30 years. If you do this, commit to repaying the car in a maximum of five years. Otherwise, I guarantee you will essentially be continually increasing the loan (you just won't see it in black and white).

Pay your debts on time – period!

You do not need to add late payment fees to your debt. Set up direct debits a few days before the due date where possible.

Repay the full amount

By paying off the entire debt, you are eliminating the need to pay interest. Over time this can add up to substantial savings, which in turn means more money in your hand.

Try to make extra repayments

Increase the amount you pay on a regular basis where possible. Another option is to direct bonus money (eg. tax refunds) to repay a lump sum off the debt. Before making lump sum repayments, ensure that you are not penalised (that there is no fee) to do so.

Review

Shop around for a better outcome. Don't just look at the interest rate when comparing options. Remember to look at the fees associated with either exiting the current option or the overall fees of (what looks like) the better option.

Don't be fooled by 'Buy Now, Pay Later'

It is still debt, so someone (not you) will always be making money. The consequences for defaulting can be extremely costly.

Fill out the debt template provided to you in the workbook.

CREATING YOUR SPENDING PLAN

Now that you have compiled all the information relating to your income and expenses, you have the foundations to create a detailed spending plan that's specific to you and your situation.

It's time to get to work on your cashflow. Without a detailed cashflow, you will continue to assume, rather than really know what is going on. The best part about building your cashflow is that if you complete it once, you will only require a few tweaks each time it is updated to keep you going. Ultimately, the goal is to have a surplus at the end of each month and then to be able to work on a plan for that surplus. By reframing the way we think about "spending plans", we can start to see them as positive tools for achieving our financial goals and living a more intentional life.

The difference I see when clients start using a cashflow is incredible. Understanding your money (at the most basic level, in terms of money coming in and going out) is empowering. There are so many templates out there to build a cashflow. You can use one you find online, create your own, or use the one in the workbook. No matter which direction you go, please find one and commit to it.

The key components of your spending plan are:

Cashflow – understanding where your money is going
You should have completed this through the spending audit section of this chapter. Revisit this to ensure you have an understanding of your essential versus non-essential spending.

Spending decisions
Often referred to as discretional spending, non-essential expenses such as eating out can eat into our cashflow and should be a focus when creating a spending plan. Make some proactive decisions as to cutting back or even cutting out some of this spending, to create a greater surplus.

Investigate more affordable options initially to give you the confidence to build your surplus. Remember, some of these expenses could be turned into rewards for meeting your goals.

Income opportunities

If you are a salaried employee, increasing your cash inflow is not a definite possibility, but you should at least ask yourself the question: do you have opportunities to increase your income?

Is it time to ask for a raise? Is overtime available? Revisit any eligibility for financial assistance or even sell items you no longer use. Maybe you have an entrepreneurial fire and can start something on the side.

If you own your business, you should be putting your own salary requirements at the top of your "to-do list". I talk about this in more detail in the next chapter.

Reducing debt

As I discussed in detail above, prioritise reducing non-deductible debt, with the highest interest rates at the top of the list – eg. credit cards.

Surplus choices

Building an emergency fund is the first priority when deciding what to do once we create a surplus in your cashflow. Having funds set aside to pay for unexpected expenses avoids you having to turn to the credit card or loans in these circumstances.

The amount to save comes down purely to your own peace of mind. It could be a multiple of your monthly expenses or just a set dollar figure. The choice is yours. Like everything, commit to it and the timeframe you give yourself to save it.

Remember, if you do need to use these funds for an unexpected expense, restart the saving component to replace the funds used. Also, ensure that you review the expense that you had to meet and decide if it is an expense that should be accounted for in your cashflow planning.

Ask for help

Seek professional advice if you feel you would benefit from further guidance about managing your money to align with your specific circumstances.

You can revisit the template we used during the spending audit to also keep track of your actual spending. This template can also be used to asses your expected surplus and assist in creating specific, and attainable cash flow goals.

Revisit the spending plan template in the workbook to record any changes you have committed to.

SPENDING GOALS

To help curb impulsive online purchases, another task you can undertake is to review your email activity from the past month, including deleted items. If you have permanently deleted any emails, make a note of them from this point forward.

Create a list of all the email subscriptions you receive and categorise them into the following groups:

- Shopping.
- Personal growth, including health.
- Finance and money.

Then, further categorise each group based on the following:

- Delete immediately.
- Briefly skim and then delete.
- File for later reference.
- Read and print out.
- Take action.

Take a moment to assess where you're spending your time and focus. If your inbox is overflowing with marketing emails instead of informative content, consider intentionally unsubscribing from some of them.

REFLECTIONS AND LESSONS

Now this was a chapter full of action. Well done!

Breaking the cycle of living payday to payday is challenging and requires a realistic spending plan, but most importantly, it requires your discipline and patience. Be kind to yourself and give yourself time to start creating healthy financial habits.

CREDIT CARD DEBT

If money is tight and you resort to using a credit card to supplement or top up your life, how do you ever expect to get ahead if you are paying between 15%-20% in interest? Make smart decisions about what credit cards you use, how you pay them off and what kind of debt you are committing to.

KEEPING UP WITH THE JONESES

Money talks and wealth whispers – in other words, don't go broke trying to look rich. Often, we are anxious or stressed when we aren't aligned with our morals and values. The same goes for our spending – make sure you are spending on what is important to you and your family. Don't go comparing yourself to others.

Now that you have completed this chapter, you may wish to go back and review chapter 2 to ensure that your spending plan aligns with your personal and financial goals and vice versa.

Creating a spending plan sets you up to achieve your financial goals as well as giving you an insight into where you may fall into the trap of overspending or falling into debt. It is an important step into taking control of your finances and your financial future.

①	②	③	④	⑤
Remember	Understand	Analyse	Apply	Extend

1. REMEMBER:

What were some of the specific skills, knowledge, or habits that you gained during this chapter?

....

....

....

....

....

....

....

2. UNDERSTAND:

Why are these accomplishments important for your financial fitness? How will they impact your life in the short-term and long-term?

3. ANALYSE:

What were some of the positive/helpful behaviours you've noticed you have? And what were some of the negative/unhelpful behaviours that you need to be aware of going forward?

REFLECTIONS & ACTIONS
4. APPLY:

Where and how can you apply the knowledge and skills you gained during this chapter? What are some of the specific areas where you can apply your new financial literacy, and how will you do so?

5. EXTEND:

How can you use the knowledge and skills you gained during this chapter in other parts of your life? How can you extend the benefits of financial fitness beyond just your personal finances?

Just as rest and recovery are critical components of physical fitness, reflection plays a vital role in becoming financially fit.

It allows us to pause, take a step back, and evaluate our progress towards our goals.

Without reflection, we risk falling into old habits and repeating the same mistakes.

By reflecting on our actions and decisions, we can gain insight into what works for us and what doesn't, and make the necessary adjustments to achieve success.

So just as we make time for stretching and warm-ups in our physical fitness routine, we must also prioritise regular reflection to keep our minds and actions aligned with our goals.

"You have the power within. It's not your past that's going to define who you are but it's what you believe about yourself; what is it that you expect from yourself."

Dr Tererai Trent

"We need to do
a better job of
putting ourselves
higher on our
"to do" list."

Michelle Obama

CHAPTER 5

MONEY AND WAGES

The Importance of Paying
Yourself a Salary

WHY YOU SHOULD START PAYING YOURSELF A SALARY

It's not selfish to pay yourself a salary. It's not a luxury. You are in business to make money, and a portion of that money should be yours to keep.

Business owners think about money constantly: how much is coming in, how much needs to be paid out, how much needs to be set aside for tax and GST, how much can be put towards marketing, how much can be socked away for emergencies... the list goes on. Does this sound familiar? If you run your own business, I'm sure it does. However, so many business owners I work with struggle with the issue of paying themselves every day. To state the obvious here: even business owners have personal bills to pay.

When money gets tight or a single financial priority rises to the surface, many business owners do one thing first: cut their own salaries. You always pay your employees, the bills, and the rent, but when cash is scarce you put off paying yourself a salary – often for longer than you should.

Trust me, I speak from experience when I say that I know how important it is to prioritise yourself.

I want you to think about what you would be earning if you were doing this as a job and being paid a full-time salary by someone else.

Questions to think about:

- What did you earn in your previous role? If you are working less hours than full-time, still work out a full-time salary, and then you can pro-rata everything.

- Do you know the current market rate for the work that you do? What would you be earning if you were working for someone else?

- What would your monthly income be for doing this job? Don't forget to break it down with figures for gross, net, super and (potentially) other allowances. Get clear on the numbers.

Your previous salary can be used as a baseline in determining how much you should be paying yourself if you own your own business.

GET CLEAR ON YOUR NUMBERS

So often, I find that my clients simply aren't charging a high enough price for their services to be able to pay themselves properly for the work that they do.

> *The percentage of women business owners I have worked with that don't pay themselves a salary is higher than 50%.*

I am on a mission to bring this number down, or at least have more women understanding how they are (or should be) financially rewarded for their own hard work within their businesses.

> *When we are clear on the numbers, we can set our pricing to support us and our business. We can pay ourselves what we deserve, to support ourselves and our families and meet our goals.*

HOW CAN YOU INCREASE WHAT YOU GET OUT OF THE BUSINESS?

Cash is key when you're running a small business. This includes invoicing your customers well. It's looking after the cash and making sure you're not burning through it on the other side of the ledger.

Think about what you anticipate spending in six to eight months, evaluate assumptions about cost of goods sold, overheads, cash collection, growth, seasonal costs in the business, when you need to invest and get inventory on hand, or if there is anything that could create a closure for you. Forecasting is important in small businesses, particularly when you're getting started. This planning means the team around you will be able to think about running the business and managing growth effectively.

We have delved into reviewing and reducing expenses throughout earlier chapters. Although there is often room for improvement, many expenses that relate to a business will always exist. And, let's be honest, the thought of cutting costs can be quite disheartening, and we find it difficult to motivate ourselves to carry out these changes.

INCREASING REVENUE

With a positive mindset, you should ask yourself: how can I increase the money that ends up in my bank account? In this section, let's spend some time on an exciting concept – increasing revenue. Businesses can increase revenue and ultimately open the door for improved profit by:

1. Raising prices.
2. Increasing the number of customers.
3. Diversifying services/product options.

Sounds simple enough, right? Problem is, we are often our own worst enemy when it comes to increasing revenue. Our mindset can make a huge impact on how we approach money.

FIVE MINDSET SHIFTS TO INCREASE REVENUE

I'm going to share with you five mindset shifts for increasing your revenue.

1. Review what you are spending your time on.

Just because you are busy, it doesn't mean you are profitable. When you have your own business, you are usually not paid by the hour, and you are most definitely not paid for all of your tasks and to-dos. You may, however, have clients that pay you by the hour. Spending all of your time trying to change something on your website or update your admin means you're not spending time on client work. You can use automation and outsourcing to free up time to focus on the things that bring in the dollars and move your business forward.

2. Clients come first.

A common mistake is to forget to focus on the most important people who are integral to your success – your customers and clients. Always ask yourself if what you are doing or planning will be beneficial to current and new clients.

3. Accept help.

One of the toughest things to do is ask for help. Although you could quite possibly be a one-woman show to start with, as your business evolves, you will want to grow your village. Seek out people (not just friends) to support you, but who will also challenge you. Accountability is often easier when you have someone else in your fold.

4. Personal development.

Don't be deterred from investing in yourself! Prioritise learning to further your knowledge. This could be directly related to your specialty (as well as your "not so great" areas) so that you can continue to grow and forge ahead as a leader in your field. If the funds aren't there yet, look at free workshops or budget in your cashflow for non-negotiables.

5. Value yourself.

Take a realistic look at what you charge. Believe in your worth. As business owners and women, we are often our own harshest critics. Do not settle for less than you are worth.

Don't be afraid to raise your rates to reflect your knowledge and time.

WHY IT'S IMPORTANT TO PAY YOURSELF

> To keep a business healthy in the long run, you must pay yourself a salary on a regular basis. Even if you're still in the start-up phase and living off personal savings, paying yourself from the beginning has advantages you can't afford to miss.

Skipping our own salaries as a financial fix isn't selfless or smart – it's unsustainable and should be considered a last-ditch effort. Here are my pros and cons to paying yourself (starting with the cons).

THE CONS OF NOT PAYING YOURSELF
Adds to your money worries/sleepless nights

When your income varies from month to month and you're the one responsible for this, you spend lots of sleepless nights fretting over personal finances.

While some worry is completely normal (and to be expected), too much will always distract you from doing what you do best – using your energy to work on your business success. If you funnel all of your profits back into the business, you will stretch your own personal finances.

Clouds your understanding of your business finances and isn't sustainable

Building your business with the illusion that success is just being able to meet operating expenses is unwise and unsustainable. Much of the money in your business account will always be spoken for by the everyday expenses. In fact, the money in the business account actually belongs to the business; it is not yours personally. Having sufficient cashflow is vital for any business, and it's far easier to manage cashflow when you have predictable expenses you can plan around, including your salary.

Everything within the business will most probably keep functioning when you are paying everyone else except yourself. However, this doesn't mean that your business is actually meeting financial goals and ultimately the success you seek. Your own salary needs to be a regular expense in the business budget. Sometimes skipping your salary is unavoidable, but constantly doing it can distort your understanding of your business financials. The point to keep in mind is that cashflow is king.

THE PROS OF PAYING YOURSELF
It's what you are used to
Think back to the days before you started your business when you were working for someone else. Chances are you were rewarded for your hard work with a regular salary. It may not have always been the same amount, but it came through like clockwork. And for the next week, month, or however often you got paid, you'd do your best to manage your expenses and make your money last. You couldn't ask your employer for more money when you ran out.

It gives you an understanding of your business's financial success
Having sufficient cashflow is vital for any business, and it's far easier to manage cashflow when you have predictable expenses you can plan around – including your salary.

Keeping ahead of the taxman

When wage and salary earners are paid, the employer must withhold and set aside a portion of their pay as tax. When you withdraw money from your business, it's not 'free money' (ie. tax-free). These amounts, depending on your business structure, need to be properly accounted for.

How you take money from your business could be building up a potential debt that will need to be paid back at some point. Furthermore, this debt could lead to severe cashflow problems down the track, especially when it comes time to sell the business. It's important to be aware of this, and pay yourself a salary, as it will help to avoid these situations.

The banks will like you more

When it comes to assessing a person's ability to service a potential loan, banks much prefer consistently earning wage and salary earners to sporadically earning self-employed business owners. The bank wants to know you can comfortably service the loan each month, and by paying yourself a regular salary, you'll have the payslips and bank statements to show a steady cashflow history. So, the sooner you set this up in your business, the better.

It is what you deserve!

Do I really need to elaborate on this one for you? Why wait any longer? Start paying yourself today!

"The biggest adventure you can take is to live the life of your dreams."

Oprah Winfrey

HOW TO PAY YOURSELF

Many business owners pay themselves in one of two ways:

1. They pay themselves a salary on the books, and have the appropriate amount of tax (and superannuation) withheld.
2. They just take whatever they want and have their accountant sort it out at the end of the year.

Have a guess at which is the most often used strategy. Yes, you guessed correctly – the second one. The main reason for this is the fear of taking too much and leaving the business with potential cashflow pressures.

And my preference? You are correct if you guessed the first option. If you want a little bonus at the end of the year, or perhaps six months into the financial year, you can pay yourself an employee bonus, a directors' fee, or even a fully franked dividend. However, this is definitely something you should speak to your accountant or advisor about first, and should be part of your planning each and every financial year.

The amount you pay yourself has a lot of variables, such as legal structure of the business (which I discussed in the previous chapter), consistency of cashflow, and the most important one, your own personal financial goals.

As a business owner, you have the freedom to determine your own salary. As your profits grow, evaluate your salary the same way you would an employee's. You have the power to pay yourself more when profits are high and less during economic downturns or when expenses arise.

How you pay yourself can depend on a number of factors:

Business structure

The type of business structure you have will determine how you can pay yourself. If you are a sole trader, you can take money out as needed. Taking money out of a company is more complex.

Legislative restrictions

You need to ensure you are complying with all relevant rules and requirements when paying yourself a salary.

Tax outcomes

You need to consider the tax outcome of your salary on the business as well as your personal tax obligations.

Commercial considerations

These include employee perception and shareholder expectations. Make sure you are always transparent with your salary when there are other shareholders involved in your business.

Peace of mind

As I have discussed, both personal and business cashflow are often causes of stress and anxiety. You need to access your comfort levels for both.

DRAWINGS VS DIVIDENDS VS SALARY
Drawings

Usually this is the first approach most small business owners take. Have you ever heard yourself say, "I can't possibly take a salary yet"? Instead, it becomes a 'take what I need, when I need it' approach. This then leads to accountants working it out at the end of the year. As much as this takes away the conscious need for planning, it is often inconsistent, which then flows through to potential issues with cashflow and future business planning. This is not a great outcome if you are wanting to develop sound business practices and create successful habits for paying yourself. The financial issues can include being unprepared for a personal tax liability once tax returns are completed; if you are a company, this approach will often lead to issues with director's loans.

Salary

Whether you are a sole trader or a company, paying yourself a salary creates consistent habits that then flow through to your personal financial planning. Consistency is favourable for any business planning, especially cashflow.

If you are trading as a company, a salary also guarantees regular superannuation contributions, as well as tax being withheld, which reduces the tax liability surprise at the end of the year. The salary and the superannuation become tax deductible expenses to the business.

Dividends

In my view, a company having the ability to pay dividends is one of the greatest measures of success. They are a game of patience and profit!

Dividends are generally tax efficient as they are paid out after tax. They represent the profits of the business that have already had tax paid (and at a lower rate than most individual salaries).

Dividends do not attract superannuation guarantee or payroll tax, which can alleviate cashflow pressures in a business. How the dividend is treated from a personal tax perspective should be discussed with your accountant.

Consider in depth all of the factors discussed above when determining the best way to pay yourself. I recommend seeking professional assistance from your bookkeeper, accountant or financial advisor, to ensure that the money you pay out as a salary is not only aligned to your personal goals but is also beneficial to the business.

HOW MUCH SHOULD I PAY MYSELF?

As you can see, there are many good reasons to pay yourself a regular salary instead of dipping into the business account on an ad hoc basis. The next question to tackle is, how much should you pay yourself?

PAY YOURSELF ENOUGH TO GET BY

Obviously, you need to pay yourself enough money to cover your basic living and lifestyle requirements. The last thing you want is to be stressed about your personal finances, especially when you're trying to make business decisions.

PAY YOURSELF WHAT YOU ARE WORTH

By paying yourself what you are worth, you will be setting a bar at market rates for the work and hours you complete. You will feel a sense of self-worth and satisfaction from being remunerated at a level you are truly worth. It also allows for future financial rewards when the business achieves beyond the budget.

It's not always a good idea to pay yourself too much in salary, even if the business can easily afford the cashflow. Similarly, if you are still in the start-up phase, reduce your overhead costs as much as possible and pay yourself a small but regular amount. Depending on your business structure, there can be more tax-effective ways to receive income from your business, such as dividends.

Every business' and person's situation is different in this regard, so it's important to get one-on-one advice in this area. Don't view this information as personal advice to you – it's not. I'm simply opening your eyes to the many benefits of paying yourself a consistent salary as a business owner.

REFLECTIONS AND LESSONS

Paying yourself shouldn't be seen as a reward for a successful business. It should be a requirement to be fairly remunerated for the work (hours and effort) that are injected into the business's success. It is important to value yourself and the role you play in your business.

Reflecting on paying yourself a salary is an important step when creating your plan for your financial fitness as you are creating the means to meet your personal goals, separate to your business goals.

① > ② > ③ > ④ > ⑤

Remember   Understand   Analyse   Apply   Extend

1. REMEMBER:

What were some of the specific skills, knowledge, or habits that you gained during this chapter?

....

....

....

....

....

2. UNDERSTAND:

Why are these accomplishments important for your financial fitness? How will they impact your life in the short-term and long-term?

3. ANALYSE:

What were some of the positive/helpful behaviours you've noticed you have? And what were some of the negative/unhelpful behaviours that you need to be aware of going forward?

REFLECTIONS & ACTIONS
4. APPLY:

Where and how can you apply the knowledge and skills you gained during this chapter? What are some of the specific areas where you can apply your new financial literacy, and how will you do so?

5. EXTEND:

How can you use the knowledge and skills you gained during this chapter in other parts of your life? How can you extend the benefits of financial fitness beyond just your personal finances?

Just as rest and recovery are critical components of physical fitness, reflection plays a vital role in becoming financially fit.

It allows us to pause, take a step back, and evaluate our progress towards our goals.

Without reflection, we risk falling into old habits and repeating the same mistakes.

By reflecting on our actions and decisions, we can gain insight into what works for us and what doesn't, and make the necessary adjustments to achieve success.

So just as we make time for stretching and warm-ups in our physical fitness routine, we must also prioritise regular reflection to keep our minds and actions aligned with our goals.

"I think the things you most regret in life are things you didn't do."

Steve Jobs

CHAPTER 6

MONEY FOR THE UNEXPECTED

Preparing for Financial Emergencies and Unexpected Expenses

UNDERSTANDING PERSONAL INSURANCE

Insurance isn't a fun topic for anyone, even as a financial advisor. However, I am known to bang on about your greatest asset being your ability to earn an income. How we protect our income comes into that. Insurance is about expecting, planning and paying for any of the gaps that would exist should an unexpected event occur. Insurance can protect your family financially from unforeseen events by providing a lump sum or continuous payment whilst you are incapacitated.

A quick personal story for you. In 2010, I found myself in intensive care in hospital. I remember nurses bringing a "crash cart", and me being rushed to get the care I required. Whilst I distinctly remember the fear of dying, I also remember a form of calm setting over me, because of I knew that I had adequate insurance to protect my girls should the worst-case scenario occur, and also that I had income protection. The fear was focused on my health and my health alone, as I wasn't concerned about any finances because my family and I were protected by insurance.

Even though so many people have a deep concern about the longevity of their funds and the overall financial security of their family, it is very rare that a client will contact me with the need for personal insurance as their main motivation. Many other professionals, such as mortgage brokers or accountants, recommend clients seek cover.

TYPES OF PERSONAL INSURANCE

Life insurance

The purpose of life insurance is that it provides a lump sum benefit to your nominated beneficiary, third party or an estate in the event of your death.

Total and permanent disability insurance

Total and permanent disability (TPD) insurance provides you with a lump sum payment in the event you become totally and permanently disabled. The key purpose of this insurance is to help you pay for medical expenses and potential renovation costs due to the changes in your lifestyle. It can also be used for lump sum funding to generate income for ongoing living expenses. The definition of TPD can vary depending on the policy, and is defined in each policy document.

Trauma/critical illness insurance

Trauma insurance provides you with a lump sum payment in the event that you are diagnosed with one of a specified range of critical illnesses or injuries. Similar to TPD insurance, the purpose of this type of insurance is to help you pay for medical expenses and supplement your income whilst you are recovering.

Income protection

Income protection, also known as salary continuation, provides you with a regular source of income should you be unable to work for a period due to sickness or injury. You can generally insure for up to 70% of your earned income. There are many variables to income protection to consider, including the waiting period (the length of time you are unable to work prior to the claim going into force) and the benefit period (the length of time you will be paid for).

Child cover

Child cover can be linked to one of your own policies and provides a lump sum benefit, should your child be diagnosed with one of a specified range of illnesses or die.

INSURANCE AUDIT

> *The purpose of reviewing our insurances is to evaluate if the insurance is adequate and appropriate for your personal circumstances at a given point in time.*

These audits will identify if there are any gaps in cover or overlay, which is common considering many people are unaware that they may hold insurance inside their superannuation funds.

The aim of the audit is to ultimately provide peace of mind with the knowledge that your family is financially secure and your assets are protected in the event of your illness or unexpected death.

Most of us will have insurance attached to our superannuation funds. Attention needs to be paid to the insurance rules in place for each individual fund. You should be reviewing your current status to confirm that you are in fact eligible to claim.

To complete the audit accurately, here is a list of information you will require:

1. Current insurance policies.
2. Current superannuation statements (hint: you will also need these for chapter 8).

You will then need to collate the following information:

- Policy type – what type of cover do you hold (life, income protection, etc.)?
- Owner of the insurance (could be yourself, your business, superannuation).
- Beneficiary (yourself, partner, children, superannuation).
- Current coverage (benefit amount).
- Benefit period – when do the policies expire?
- Premium (cost of cover, frequency of payments and source of payment).
- Exclusions – are there any listed exclusions?

Fill out your insurance audit template provided for you in the workbook.

INSURANCE GOALS

Consider your own personal and financial circumstances. What would happen if you became unable to work and don't have an income for an extended period of time? What happens if you live on your own? What happens to your kids? What happens to mortgage repayments? How would you fund out-of-pocket medical expenses?

> *There's a fine line for everyone between the peace of mind of cover and the cost of that cover. For that reason, I spend time going through a needs analysis with my clients.*

The need for insurance tends to be linked to our stage of life. Often as we get older, we have dependents (eg. a family) and we take on debt for a period of time. We are starting to build our assets, including superannuation. At this point in time, our need for insurance increases. As we get older, the need to support our children (dependents) decreases. As we work and age, our superannuation balances increase, and our asset prices can increase and hopefully our debt levels decrease. Our insurance levels and needs should also decrease.

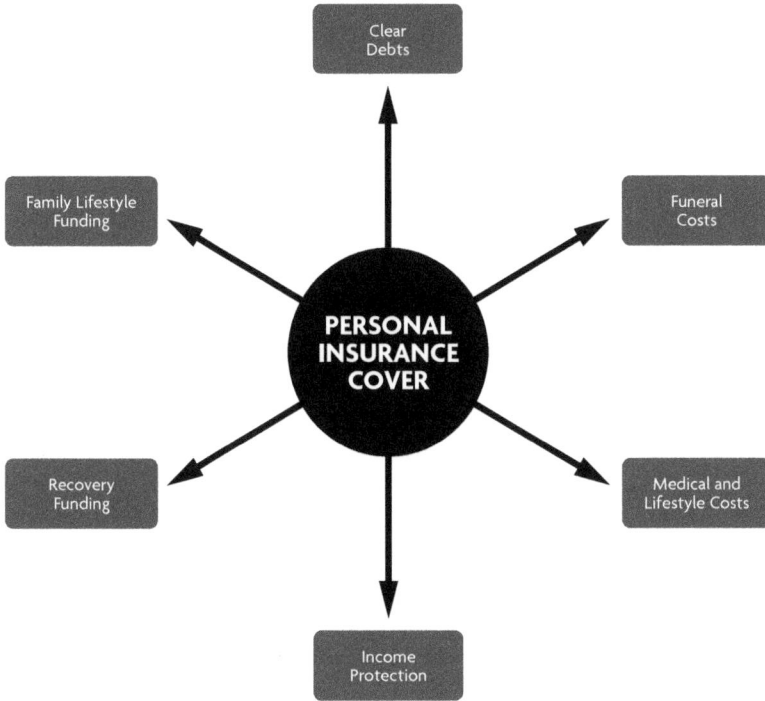

HOW MUCH INSURANCE DO I NEED?

You should consider the following when determining your insurance needs:

- **Current financial obligations** – list your current debts, such as mortgage, car loans and credit cards.

- **Future financial obligations** – a lump sum requirement, such as home modifications, children's education, funeral expenses.

- **Income replacement** – how much of your income would your family require to maintain their standard of living in the event of your inability to work, or if you pass away?

- **Existing provisions** – how much cover do you currently have?

- **Realised assets** – list the assets you have that would be realised in the event of your disablement or death, such as cash holdings, superannuation and other investments.

You can go through the needs analysis for yourself and see where the figures lie in your own insurance plans. It's important to take the time to make sure you have an understanding of what's available, your particular situation and what your needs could be.

Fill out your analysis template provided for you in the workbook.

REFLECTIONS AND LESSONS

① > ② > ③ > ④ > ⑤
Remember   Understand   Analyse   Apply   Extend

1. REMEMBER:

What were some of the specific skills, knowledge, or habits that you gained during this chapter?

2. UNDERSTAND:

Why are these accomplishments important for your financial fitness? How will they impact your life in the short-term and long-term?

3. ANALYSE:

What were some of the positive/helpful behaviours you've noticed you have? And what were some of the negative/unhelpful behaviours that you need to be aware of going forward?

REFLECTIONS & ACTIONS
4. APPLY:

Where and how can you apply the knowledge and skills you gained during this chapter? What are some of the specific areas where you can apply your new financial literacy, and how will you do so?

5. EXTEND:

How can you use the knowledge and skills you gained during this chapter in other parts of your life? How can you extend the benefits of financial fitness beyond just your personal finances?

Just as rest and recovery are critical components of physical fitness, reflection plays a vital role in becoming financially fit.

It allows us to pause, take a step back, and evaluate our progress towards our goals.

Without reflection, we risk falling into old habits and repeating the same mistakes.

By reflecting on our actions and decisions, we can gain insight into what works for us and what doesn't, and make the necessary adjustments to achieve success.

So just as we make time for stretching and warm-ups in our physical fitness routine, we must also prioritise regular reflection to keep our minds and actions aligned with our goals.

"True happiness...
is not attained
through self-
gratification, but
through fidelity
to a worthy
purpose."

Helen Keller

"It's not about how much money you make, but how much money you keep, how hard it works for you and how many generations you keep it for."

Robert Kiyosaki

CHAPTER 7

MONEY FOR TOMORROW

Investing for Long-Term Wealth
Creation and Financial Security

UNDERSTANDING INVESTING

> *Investing involves making informed decisions and sometimes accepting risk by allocating these funds into an asset that has the potential to appreciate in value over time or provide a steady income stream.*

Are you currently *thinking* about investments? In Chapter 4, Money for Today, we talked about identifying if you have a surplus in your spending plan. Now we are going to talk about rounding out the plan by allocating some or even all of the surplus to investments. The expectation of investments is that we are saving money for "tomorrow" – making a profit from generating an income in the future.

In this chapter, we will discuss how investing is a key strategy for building long-term wealth and look at the fundamentals of investing.

YOUR INVESTMENTS

If you own your own home, or you're on the way to owning it (it's mortgaged), this will most probably be the highest-valued asset for you. The big thing about houses that I want to cover, however, is that a house is never going to actually provide us with an income unless we sell it. A lot of people put a lot of money into houses, but it's important to think about the big picture.

Please remember from the insurance chapter – your most important investment is in yourself, because your ability to earn an income is your number one asset at this point in time.

Part of this big picture is that it's our home and we have an emotional attachment. Think about when you purchased it. What were the driving factors for the purchase? Was it to be in a specific schooling zone? Did you fall in love with the view? Rarely will most people's consideration be skewed to the long-term financial benefit of owning a bricks-and-mortar asset. For the longer term, the only way we can reap the rewards of our own home is to sell it; otherwise, we're just building up an estate to leave to our children. As such, if you have a house, it is an asset, but it's not giving you an income like an investment property would.

The majority of you will have superannuation, so therefore you've also invested in shares. Superannuation is a funny one, because people don't often talk about it until they get closer to retirement. They see it as something that's 'wasted' money. I'll talk about this more in the next chapter, but for now, remember it is your money and you need to pay attention to it.

Last but definitely not least is your business. Later on in the book, we'll talk about what the long-term business plan is for the growth of your business, and how you can maximise this as an asset and advantage.

INVESTMENT AUDIT

Overall, it is important to conduct regular reviews of your existing investments to ensure that your portfolio is still aligned with your values and personal financial goals, is performing well relative to benchmarks, is cost effective and is structured for current market conditions.

Make a list of the investments you currently have, including the purchase price, date of purchase, current value and any debt associated with the asset.

You can fill out the investment audit template in the workbook.

- Long-term goals
  - » Do your current investments align with your long-term financial goals?

- Performance
  - » Analyse the performance of your current assets. This allows you to identify which assets are performing or underperforming.
  - » What is the overall growth of your asset? Calculate this in both dollar terms and as a percentage.

Growth in Dollars = Final Value – Initial Investment

Growth in Percentage = (Growth in Dollars/Initial Investment) x 100

Annual Growth as a Percentage = Growth in Percentage/Years of Investment

» How does that compare to any relevant benchmark?

» Does your asset provide you with an income? Again, calculate this in both dollar terms and as a percentage.

Note: we will go into superannuation in depth in the following chapter, so for now it is okay to just list the value of superannuation. There is no need to complete a full audit at this stage.

• Fees

» Outline all of the fees associated with your investment.

• Your circumstances

» Has any of your personal circumstances changed? For example, has there been the need to decrease your investment timeframe? If so, you may need to adjust your portfolio to decrease short-term risk.

INVESTMENT GOALS

If you think about your current investments, what does financial success look like to you?

When we consider this, we're thinking back to the start of this book, when we talked about our goals and dreams for money, and what money can do for you in the long-term.

The other questions to ask yourself are: how will you fund investments? Is it superannuation? Is it paying off your home loan? Is it a lump sum that you have to invest? Are you going to start a regular investment plan?

Again, going back to the beginning of the book, what's holding you back in your money mindset? What is actually holding you back from starting an active investment plan?

The other investment opportunities that we have, other than what we've just spoken about, are: high interest term deposits, investment properties, and shares outside of superannuation. There is a wealth of opportunities, it's just about what you are comfortable with and what works for you.

You can find a template in the workbook to record your investment goals.

KEY COMPONENTS OF A SUCCESSFUL INVESTMENT STRATEGY

Knowledge

Whether you are just starting out or invest regularly, it is important to continually build on the knowledge and skills you have, because the financial markets, regulations, economic events and options available to you are constantly evolving.

The suitability of one investment can differ from person to person and therefore there is no "one-size-fits-all" approach. You need to assess your own personal situation and then make an informed decision.

Risk profile

The most significant thing to think about is your attitude to risk, or your risk profile. It is your personal tolerance to accepting risk associated with investing. Often when talking about investing, people will say, "What's your tolerance for losing money?" Your risk profile is influenced by a number of factors including your timeframe, your previous experience with investing, your current financial situation and, yes, your reaction to loss.

By completing a risk profile, you are able to gain an insight into your own tolerance, and then find an investment that has the right balance between risk and return that is suited to you.

Curious about your risk tolerance when it comes to investing? Just type 'Investment Risk Tolerance Assessment, Missouri University' into your search engine. This is a bit of a fun questionnaire.

Timeframe

What is your timeframe? You may have heard of "time in the market, not timing the market", because investments of any sort can be volatile. Determining your timeframe is essential as it impacts the investments that are most suitable to you and the level of risk you can take on within your timeframe.

Liquidity

Liquidity refers to how easily an asset or investment can be sold. Take a house for example. Firstly, you can't sell brick by brick, so therefore you will have to sell the whole house. The timeframe of this is also quite long when you consider advertising as well as settlement time. On the other hand, shares can usually be sold within a day, during trading hours.

Ownership

You should also consider ownership and entity – are you going to own any assets or investments? Is it through companies or family trusts in your name? Or your kids' names? Is it superannuation?

Then, consider what you want from the investment. For example, with owning a home, the majority of us won't be renting out part of our home, so our homes are growth only. Shared bank accounts will be income only, as the value of your money grows by the income that it generates.

Tax implications

Often tax implications and ownership are closely related. Potential tax implications should be considered when deciding on the ownership structure. What are the tax implications? There might be capital gains tax or income tax.

Consideration should be given to the asset and if it will be income-generating, and therefore an ongoing income tax issue or growth-orientated, which could result in capital gains tax on sale of the asset. Timing of selling also needs to be considered alongside tax considerations.

Patience

As I stated earlier, investing should be seen as a long-term focus. Unless you are a day trader, it is not about getting rich quickly, but more about developing a long-term habit to increase your wealth.

Patience is also important, so you are not making impulsive decisions. This is particularly relevant if you're investing in shares or other assets, subject to market volatility. The last thing you want to do is make a hasty decision to sell something and make a significant loss, only to find the value increases again.

Your legacy

Think about: when do you want to spend that money? How much do you want to leave for your children? Is it going to go into a family trust? Do you want to protect it? There are a lot of questions to ask.

INVESTMENT OPPORTUNITIES
Cash

Cash is the most liquid investment. It includes your physical cash holdings, as well as bank transaction and savings accounts. These are income only investments and usually offer low interest rates, but do not lose capital value (apart from the effects of inflation) and are therefore a good option for short-term investment, such as an emergency fund.

Term deposits

Term deposits are a fixed-term investment with a set interest rate for the period you select. Terms available usually range from one month to five years and will generally have a higher interest rate than cash accounts. You may incur penalty costs if you break a term deposit early.

Commodities

You can buy physical commodities such as gold, silver and platinum in the form of coins or bullion. You can either store this yourself or pay for storage. This form of investment provides capital growth only. To sell physical commodities you need to approach a dealer or broker to find a buyer.

Property

You can invest in property directly, by purchasing an investment property or through a real estate investment trust (REIT). Property offers capital growth when you sell your property or units in an REIT. You also receive an income from property, through rent received or distributions from the REIT.

The main differences between owning a property directly and units in an REIT are liquidity and expenses. As I discussed earlier, to realise the capital growth in a property, the entire property needs to be sold whereas units held in an REIT can be partially sold. Rental property expenses need to be accounted for by the owner, whereas within an REIT, all expenses are calculated prior to returns being given.

Shares

You can invest in shares directly via share trading platforms, or through a managed fund. Managed funds pool investors' money together to purchase shares in companies. When you invest in managed funds you buy units in the funds which allows the investor access to a diversified range of shares.

Shares and managed funds offer capital growth, where you sell the share for higher than your purchase price and income through dividends, which is a portion of the company's profits that are paid out to the shareholders.

Managed funds have the added benefit of professional knowledge, as the fund manager makes decisions on what stocks to buy and sell and when to make transactions. However, this does increase the fees associated with investing this way, compared to direct shares.

CURRENT INVESTMENT TRENDS
MICRO-INVESTING PLATFORMS

A micro-investing platform is an application that allows users to regularly save small sums of money. Micro-investing platforms aim to remove traditional barriers to investing, such as brokerage account minimums, and encourage people to invest even if they have limited incomes and assets.

Key takeaways

- By making investing simple and painless, micro-investing platforms can help people who otherwise wouldn't accumulate savings for future investment.
- These platforms take tiny amounts of money, usually from rounding up transactions, and invest them into exchange-traded funds-based accounts.
- Small savings can add up over time to yield returns that beat traditional savings vehicles like a savings account or a certificate of deposit.

CRYPTOCURRENCY

"Cryptocurrencies are digital tokens. They are a type of digital currency that allows people to make payments directly to each other through an online system. Cryptocurrencies have no legislated or intrinsic value; they are simply worth what people are willing to pay for them in the market. This is in contrast to national currencies, which get part of their value from being legislated as legal tender. There are a number of cryptocurrencies – the most well-known of these are Bitcoin and Ether."[2]

Key takeaways

- There is currently no controlling body for cryptocurrency.
- Transferring cryptocurrency between parties is both speedy and cost-effective.
- Crypto is an extremely volatile market that is inundated with currencies.

EXCHANGE-TRADED FUNDS (ETFS)

"Exchange-traded funds (ETFs) are a low-cost way to earn a return similar to an index or a commodity. They can also help to diversify your investments. You can buy and sell units in ETFs through a stockbroker, the same way you buy and sell shares. An ETF is a managed fund that you can buy or sell on an exchange, like the Australian Securities Exchange (ASX). In Australia, most ETFs are passive investments that don't try to outperform the market. The role of the fund manager is to track the value of an index, for example the ASX200 or S&P500 [or] a specific commodity, such as gold. The value of the ETF goes up or down with the index or asset they're tracking."[3]

Key takeaways

- ETFs trade like an individual share on the Australian Securities Exchange, our stock exchange.
- Price is continuously calculated throughout the day.
- The ETF offerings are increasing across all sectors.
- ETFs are low-cost due to being directly linked to an index. This means that no decision-making by managers is required.

REFLECTIONS AND LESSONS

This chapter is an exciting one because we get to start focusing on wealth creation and achieving our financial goals.

Remember, each investment option available has unique characteristics and varying risk and return. It is important to understand the differences and how they will suit your investment goals.

Investing can be overwhelming, but my number one piece of advice is to start small but start somewhere. Revisit your goals from chapter 2 and use your risk profile to create your investment strategy.

① > ② > ③ > ④ > ⑤

Remember   Understand   Analyse   Apply   Extend

1. REMEMBER:

What were some of the specific skills, knowledge, or habits that you gained during this chapter?

....

....

....

....

....

2. UNDERSTAND:

Why are these accomplishments important for your financial fitness? How will they impact your life in the short-term and long-term?

3. ANALYSE:

What were some of the positive/helpful behaviours you've noticed you have? And what were some of the negative/unhelpful behaviours that you need to be aware of going forward?

....

....

....

....

....

....

....

....

....

....

....

....

....

REFLECTIONS & ACTIONS
4. APPLY:

Where and how can you apply the knowledge and skills you gained during this chapter? What are some of the specific areas where you can apply your new financial literacy, and how will you do so?

5. EXTEND:

How can you use the knowledge and skills you gained during this chapter in other parts of your life? How can you extend the benefits of financial fitness beyond just your personal finances?

Just as rest and recovery are critical components of physical fitness, reflection plays a vital role in becoming financially fit.

It allows us to pause, take a step back, and evaluate our progress towards our goals.

Without reflection, we risk falling into old habits and repeating the same mistakes.

By reflecting on our actions and decisions, we can gain insight into what works for us and what doesn't, and make the necessary adjustments to achieve success.

So just as we make time for stretching and warm-ups in our physical fitness routine, we must also prioritise regular reflection to keep our minds and actions aligned with our goals.

"If you don't find
a way to make
money while you
sleep, you will
work until you die."

Warren Buffett

CHAPTER 8

MONEY FOR RETIREMENT

Maximising Your Superannuation and
Creating a Retirement Plan for
a Comfortable Future

UNDERSTANDING SUPERANNUATION

A lot of us don't consider superannuation to be important, because we can't touch it for so long and the government has control over it. But the fact is that for most of us, our superannuation will be our second most valuable asset after the family home.

> *Superannuation is mandatory in Australia, as it the key to funding our income in retirement.*

This is why it's so heavily regulated and has so many rules attached to it. The government wants us to be self-supported retirees and there will be no pension for the majority of us, and that's a hard thing to comprehend because it is so far away.

> *My opinion is, no matter which government is in, no matter where we see superannuation in Australia, super will always be the most tax-effective vehicle for us to fund our retirement. This means that we need to have a plan.*

There are lots of different things to consider when it comes to superannuation. I will go into some of the essential information required to understand superannuation and you will find a more detailed glossary of superannuation terms at the end of the book.

CONTRIBUTIONS

As I stated earlier, if you are an employee, superannuation is mandatory in Australia. Your employer must regularly contribute a set percentage of your wage to your superannuation fund. This is currently 10.5% and set to increase gradually to 12% by 2025. This is known as superannuation guarantee (SG).

In addition to this, you are able to increase your concessional (taxed) contribution, most commonly through salary sacrifice, to a maximum of $27,500 (which includes your SG contribution). You can also add to your superannuation with "after tax" funds, known as non-concessional contributions. The current annual cap for these contributions is $110,000.

TAX CONCESSIONS

Superannuation contributions and earnings are taxed at a concessional rate of 15%, which is often lower than most people's marginal tax rate. When your fund is in retirement phase (pension), the tax rate reduces to zero. There can be significant tax savings over time if you have a sound contribution strategy in place.

INVESTMENT

Most superannuation funds offer a range of investment options, including diversified portfolios which give you access to most asset classes. As you can't withdraw your money, all income derived from your "investments" is reinvested back into the fund and ultimately benefit from compound growth.

ACCESSING SUPERANNUATION

When you retire and reach your preservation age (currently between 58 and 60), you can access your superannuation either as a lump sum or as a regular income stream. There are some exceptional circumstances, such as permanent disability or severe financial hardship, where you may be able to access your superannuation prior to your preservation age.

PROTECTION

Superannuation sits external to your will and therefore, as long as you have named a valid beneficiary, the proceeds of your superannuation can be transferred directly to the individual(s) without the need to go through probate.

An additional note is that your superannuation is protected against creditors in the event of bankruptcy.

Later in this chapter, I've included a range of online tools and resources for you to use and consider. I've also included a range of tools and reference material for you throughout the chapter, to set you up in the best way possible.

Don't get overwhelmed by this information. You don't need to use everything or look into all of the online calculators. Instead, start with the ones that are most relevant or most interesting to you at this time, and come back to the others later.

SUPERANNUATION AUDIT

It is time to take control of your retirement savings and make informed decisions in regard to your superannuation. It is important to review your superannuation regularly to ensure it aligns with your personal financial goals and current situation. Most superannuation products are fairly similar, and it is important to choose a fund based on the investment options, insurance quality and applicable fees. Like any audit, the aim is to identify any gaps or areas for improvement.

Here are some steps to follow to complete your personal audit.

Documents to gather:
- Recent payslip (ensure year-to-date figures are included).
- All superannuation statements (including any old funds you know of). You can log in to your MyGov account to obtain a list of superannuation funds that are known to you.

If you have several superannuation funds, you may wish to consider consolidating these into a single fund. The questions below will assist you to review your holdings and determine which fund is the most appropriate for you.

Questions to consider:

- Contributions
  - » Is your employer paying your superannuation guarantee regularly?
  - » Is the correct percentage being paid?
  - » Are you making any additional contributions from your salary?
  - » Have all rollovers from other funds been received?

- Investment option(s)
  - » Make a list of the investment(s). Consider if these are in line with your investment timeline and risk tolerance.
  - » Obtain the most recent performance of your fund(s). Compare this performance against relevant benchmarks.

- Insurance cover
  - » What insurance cover do you have?
  - » Is the level of cover appropriate and accurate to your circumstances? Often we have income protection cover attached to our superannuation that has limited benefit periods.

- Beneficiary
  - » Have you nominated a beneficiary?
  - » Is the beneficiary valid? What is their relationship to you?

- Fees
  - » What are the administration and management fees of the fund(s)?

» Are there any additional fees related to your fund(s)?

» Compare these fees to similar funds.

- Lost super
  » Use the Australian Taxation Office (ATO) tools to do a quick search of any lost super that may be yours.

Learn more about superannuation and fill out your superannuation audit worksheet in the workbook.

RETIREMENT GOALS

Retirement might seem like a distant goal at the moment. However, thinking about the future is going to benefit you, both now and in the long-term. Unless you are close to retirement (within the next 5 years), I would encourage you to exclude any calculations regarding your eligibility for the age pension. Here are some specific points to get you thinking about your goals.

- Age – have you thought about what age you would like to retire at? How many years do you have remaining to accumulate your desired retirement savings?
- Lifestyle – what does life look like for you in retirement? (Think hobbies, travel, grandkids – just to name a few).
- Income required – thinking about the lifestyle you would like, what costs are associated with this? Add this to your expected everyday expenses, including healthcare.

- Debts – will you still have any significant debts when you retire?
- Source of income – what assets are you intending to derive your retirement income from? This could include superannuation, investment property, shares or other sources of income.

Now you need to ask yourself: is there a "gap"? If there is, think about if you are going to investigate the options available to you to bridge the gap and achieve your goals.

- Contribution strategy – what is your plan to achieve your superannuation goal? What strategy is most beneficial to you? And how does that strategy affect your cash flow in the present day? Overall, salary sacrifice is great ongoing solution to boosting your superannuation savings as early as possible. The benefits include lowering your taxable income, minimal effect on your net (in hand) salary, as well as compounding interest by starting as early as possible. There are other contribution options, such as spouse contributions and the government co-contribution, that you should investigate too.
- Risk profile – just as we discussed in chapter 7, Money for Tomorrow, an appropriate investment strategy is dependent on a variety of factors, which all form your risk profile. It is essential to assess your individual tolerance to risk and return, to ensure you are comfortable with the investment option(s) your superannuation is held in.

- Specific investment parameters – choose the investment options that align with your risk profile as well as any other considerations you may have. For example, sustainable investing may be important to you.
- Seek advice – if you are unsure or want some further guidance, seek out a financial advisor to assist you with the most appropriate strategies for you and your specific situation.

Now you have spent time assessing your goals, you may find some of the following tools and resources useful to ascertain how you are tracking to achieving these goals. Remember, you need to review your retirement goals regularly as your circumstances change, and you may need to adjust your plan accordingly.

SUPERANNUATION TOOLS AND RESOURCES: USEFUL SUPERANNUATION CALCULATORS

How much super should you have now?

If you want to know how much super you should have today to be on track for a "comfortable" retirement, check out SuperGuru's Super Detective tool.

How much super will you have when you retire?

Canstar's Superannuation and Retirement Planner calculator can estimate how much super you will have when you retire.

How long will your superannuation last?

AustralianSuper's Super Projection Calculator tool estimates how long your superannuation will last in retirement, if you draw your required income. It can also calculate the difference that will be made through making some small changes to your contributions now.

What is the best way to top up your super?

There are a number of ways you can add to your super, but which one is the best fit for your circumstances? Industry SuperFunds' Super Contribution Calculator compares several of these options.

There are many other calculators that can be found online; however, it is important to ensure they are generated from a reputable source as well as having the capacity to adjust parameters to meet your individual circumstances.

As well as utilising the calculators you can find online, a template inside the workbook will help you to record your goals and future contribution plans. Set your own powerful super goals in the workbook.

MY TOP THREE SUPERANNUATION TIPS

1. It's YOUR money so it SHOULD matter.
2. You should have a contribution strategy.
3. As superannuation sits outside of a will, ensure you have nominated a valid beneficiary.

Tip 1: It's your money, so it should matter

My first tip is that it's still your money, whether it is locked away or not – so you should be paying attention to what you can do with your money now and where it is, so that it can benefit you best in the future. I've given you the tools to review your current superannuation; use them to take the time to get your head around superannuation and make some decisions about where you want your superannuation to be invested, how you want it to be invested, and how you want it to be used for yourself and your future.

Tip 2: You should have a contribution strategy

The second tip is that I want you to develop some form of plan, a contribution strategy, for superannuation and the concept of saving for your retirement. There are often conversations about the tax deductibility of superannuation, and often accountants tell you to make a super contribution for that quick tax deduction.

However, I think it has to be carefully considered for the length of time that we've got until we can use that money, and also the tax considerations. If you make a tax-deductible contribution in any way, shape or form, you're still paying 15% tax into superannuation, so as small business owners, we can often control what our tax bracket is. You can be very mindful of the tax you pay or the money you 'lose' going into superannuation.

There are also often other avenues to take. I'm very big on investing outside of your business, and I'm also quite happy to invest outside superannuation. This is about having a contribution strategy for the long-term.

Tip 3: Nominate a valid beneficiary

The third tip is that you need to ensure that you have a valid beneficiary nominated on your superannuation. It's important to consider making a binding death benefit nomination, so you can have control over who gets your super. Superannuation sits outside of a will (I will explain this further in the estate planning section). If you don't have a will in place, then your super trustee decides which dependent gets your super.

You need to specifically state who your super will be distributed to and how it will be distributed to the trustee upon your death. You also need to be aware of who you can legitimately give your superannuation to. You can only give superannuation to a super dependent, which includes a spouse, a child, or someone in an interdependent relationship with yourself or your legal personal representative.

Sometimes your superannuation might own your life insurance, so your life insurance is taken out as part of your superannuation. In this case, if you've done a binding death benefit nomination, your life insurance will go in accordance with that nomination.

There may be some instances (particularly if you've got a self-managed super fund) where it's not appropriate to make one, and I'd suggest getting specialist advice about whether or not you should personally make a binding death benefit nomination.

REFLECTIONS AND LESSONS

(1) > (2) > (3) > (4) > (5)

Remember   Understand   Analyse   Apply   Extend

1. REMEMBER:

What were some of the specific skills, knowledge, or habits that you gained during this chapter?

2. UNDERSTAND:

Why are these accomplishments important for your financial fitness? How will they impact your life in the short-term and long-term?

3. ANALYSE:

What were some of the positive/helpful behaviours you've noticed you have? And what were some of the negative/unhelpful behaviours that you need to be aware of going forward?

REFLECTIONS & ACTIONS
4. APPLY:

Where and how can you apply the knowledge and skills you gained during this chapter? What are some of the specific areas where you can apply your new financial literacy, and how will you do so?

5. EXTEND:

How can you use the knowledge and skills you gained during this chapter in other parts of your life? How can you extend the benefits of financial fitness beyond just your personal finances?

Just as rest and recovery are critical components of physical fitness, reflection plays a vital role in becoming financially fit.

It allows us to pause, take a step back, and evaluate our progress towards our goals.

Without reflection, we risk falling into old habits and repeating the same mistakes.

By reflecting on our actions and decisions, we can gain insight into what works for us and what doesn't, and make the necessary adjustments to achieve success.

So just as we make time for stretching and warm-ups in our physical fitness routine, we must also prioritise regular reflection to keep our minds and actions aligned with our goals.

"Success is not a destination, it's a journey. The moment you stop trying, you fail."

Zig Ziglar

CHAPTER 9

MONEY WHEN YOU SELL YOUR BUSINESS

The Importance of Creating a Small Business Retirement Plan

YOUR LONG-TERM PLAN

Let's think about your long-term plan.

Have you considered your retirement plan for your small business? I'm happy to share mine, as it's tied to my definition of success. I can't imagine stopping what I do, so my current long-term goal is to create a safety net for myself through profits from my Financially Fit Women course and other income streams. This will allow me to have more time for other important pursuits, such as supporting survivors of domestic violence or women who lack financial literacy. My small business retirement plan involves dedicating a few days each week to volunteering, without the need for additional income. Of course, this is a personal example, and your plan may differ.

So, it's time to take a moment to think about what it is that you want for you, your family, and what the big picture is for you and your business. If this big picture is to scale up, then you need to be mindful of your books as you get closer to a time when you want to sell your business, as people aren't necessarily going to buy a business that's not profitable.

The other thing about selling a business is that I can 100% guarantee that any future purchaser will be looking at what the owner is drawing out of it, which is probably paying yourself a salary that's decent and has been growing throughout the years. A potential buyer is actually going to look at what is happening right now. It could be a passive income that they're buying, so think about that as well.

This has come full circle from the start of this, when I encouraged you to pay yourself a salary, to how this will benefit your financials in the long-term.

Take some time to think about your own long-term goals for your business. Do you intend on selling? On working to the end? Do you want to grow to give back? It's your business, so build it to suit your goals.

Here are some questions to get you started:
- What is the long-term plan for you?
- Are you building it to pay you really well?
- Are you building it to sell?
- Is your business your only asset?
- What is your exit plan?
- What is the ultimate goal of the business?

> *Every end goal is different; it's about what you want and how you are going to reach your goals.*

"If you don't know where you are going, you will probably end up somewhere else."

Lawrence J Peter

SMALL BUSINESS RETIREMENT PLAN

When I speak with small business owners, they consistently tell me that they can't figure out what the future of their business looks like. They struggle to imagine one year from now, let alone three, or five, or retirement.

I want you to spend some time reflecting on the year that has been, what you have learnt from this book and where you are going to take your business into the next year.

You have to think about what your business is going to do for you long-term, or what you want your business to look like when retirement looms. Again, I want to stress that I don't mean retirement as in retirement age, just what does the end of your business look like for you?

I have a client who had put all of his hard work into his business that he shared with his wife. Unfortunately, later in life they have decided to go their separate ways. The problem they have uncovered is that the only asset that both of them really have is this business. So, there are alarm bells here – please don't fall into this trap. This is why I emphasise superannuation, investments, investing outside of your business and building lots of sources of wealth.

So, what we're faced with now is the post-COVID business struggles. My client is trying to figure out how to buy his ex-wife out of the business so that he can continue the business. However, what we're doing now is declining the value of the business and thinking about where it's going to grow in the future, so this particular client's long-term retirement plan has been thwarted by the fact that we've got to sell some of the business in the meantime.

Some of the things that really need to be considered to avoid these situations are the structure of your business and shareholders. The shareholders are really important, especially if you're a Proprietary (Pty) Limited (Ltd) Company, investing outside of the business. I'm not just saying if relationships break down, as there are also other involuntary-type retirement options. What happens if you can no longer work? What are your modes of funding other than insurance? What is the business going to provide for you and how are you going to do it? Are the fail-safes doing well? We all need a backup plan.

> The main backup plan is that our business should be working for us, but we also need to have a vision of what our business is, what the features of the business are, and what our own personal long-term goals are. We need to take control of our businesses.

THINK ABOUT THE FUTURE FROM THE START

As I said earlier, it's important to think about how you're going to get out of the business in the future, if that is your goal. So, the trading entity seems to be buying and selling wealth out of the business each year, through salary or maybe taking the profits out on an after-tax basis, and investing in a separate investment vehicle to prepare for the future. You're working hard, so you should be able to get what you want out of the business.

This is where having the right structure from the beginning will help, if you think about how it's going to profit you and how it allows for the business to be sold in the future. Some business structures allow you to sell your contract and realise a lot of value, whereas other types of businesses allow you to bring in partners who can progress the business and bring their own consumers in. Make sure you have the right shareholders agreement, so you can decide on the right path for the business or let someone else approach the business with a well-thought-out methodology that's feasible.

REFLECTIONS AND LESSONS

1 > 2 > 3 > 4 > 5

Remember Understand Analyse Apply Extend

1. REMEMBER:

What were some of the specific skills, knowledge, or habits that you gained during this chapter?

2. UNDERSTAND:

Why are these accomplishments important for your financial fitness? How will they impact your life in the short-term and long-term?

3. ANALYSE:

What were some of the positive/helpful behaviours you've noticed you have? And what were some of the negative/unhelpful behaviours that you need to be aware of going forward?

REFLECTIONS & ACTIONS
4. APPLY:

Where and how can you apply the knowledge and skills you gained during this chapter? What are some of the specific areas where you can apply your new financial literacy, and how will you do so?

5. EXTEND:

How can you use the knowledge and skills you gained during this chapter in other parts of your life? How can you extend the benefits of financial fitness beyond just your personal finances?

Just as rest and recovery are critical components of physical fitness, reflection plays a vital role in becoming financially fit.

It allows us to pause, take a step back, and evaluate our progress towards our goals.

Without reflection, we risk falling into old habits and repeating the same mistakes.

By reflecting on our actions and decisions, we can gain insight into what works for us and what doesn't, and make the necessary adjustments to achieve success.

So just as we make time for stretching and warm-ups in our physical fitness routine, we must also prioritise regular reflection to keep our minds and actions aligned with our goals.

"I've learned that people will forget what you said, people will forget what you did, but people will never forget how you made them feel."

Maya Angelou

CHAPTER 10

MONEY FOR YOUR FAMILY

Creating a Financial Plan to Provide
for Your Loved Ones and
Protect Their Future

ESTATE PLANNING

Do you recall the personal story I told you in chapter 6? Quick recall, the one where I found myself in intensive care? I had a sense of calm because I knew my insurances were adequate and that if indeed I didn't last this test, that my two girls would be financially supported. What I didn't mention in that chapter, was the fact that although I had separated from my husband, I hadn't quite gotten around (nor made it a priority) to change my will and other important estate planning facets. In this case, that situation would see my *ex*-husband making decisions about my health and medical treatment, as well as being the beneficiary of my estate. The result in this instance was an emergency call to my lawyer to rewrite my will and power of attorney by the side of my ICU bed. So, this is one of the times where my lesson is most definitely to do as I suggest and not as I did.

Unfortunately, I can attest to the fact that death, money and emotion often do not mix well.

> *To me, estate planning is you actually protecting those you love by explaining your wishes clearly, in a way that can be executed without further stress or emotion for your family.*

Through 20 years of being a financial advisor, I have now been involved with many estate issues. I have lost two clients during this time and one in particular devasted me, as he was also a friend. However, he felt secure as we were able to plan ahead to set things up correctly, to ensure his wife and two children were cared for financially in the most effective way.

UNDERSTANDING ESTATE PLANNING

In the words of the great Benjamin Franklin, "In this world, nothing can be said to be certain, except death and taxes." It's great to have insurance for all sorts of things that may or may not happen – such as car insurance, home insurance and health insurance – but it is an estate plan that ensures your assets are distributed to the people that you'd like, in the way that you'd like and in the most financially prudent manner.

WHAT IS AN ESTATE PLAN?

An estate plan is essentially a plan that provides protection to you and your family over your assets. The ultimate goal of an estate plan is to detail how you want your assets distributed and to whom, in the event of your death. It is important for everyone, regardless of the number of and value of their estate, as it ensures that your wishes are followed so that your loved ones are cared for and provided for in the event you pass away.

An estate plan is more than just a will. It should also include an enduring power of attorney for financial and personal matters, as well as an appointment of a decision-maker about medical treatment and/or financial matters in the event of your incapacity. Other inclusions to your estate plan can be a binding death benefit nomination in respect to your superannuation, succession planning arrangements in respect to any trust or company that you are a controlling person in, and any other agreements which touch upon your estate plan, such as a prenup.

DYING WITHOUT A WILL

If you die without a valid will, you are said to have died "intestate", and your estate will be distributed in accordance with a set formula, set out under the laws of the state in which you pass. In real terms, you lose the chance to decide who gets your estate and in what proportions.

There are often more legal costs in respect to dying intestate, and it can take a lot longer to distribute your estate because of additional legal processes.

Without your wishes being recorded, often this can lead to disagreements amongst family members (remember, money and emotion do not mix well) which can lead to complications and disputes that require further legal advice (and fees) to the estate.

CAN I WRITE MY OWN WILL?

The short answer is yes, you can write your own will. However, like many do-it-yourself jobs in life, there's often much more to it than you expect. A minor home reno that you've undertaken yourself is going to show its defects pretty quickly, but unfortunately, you're not going to know how bad your job is in respect to your will until it's too late.

Some of the common problems with homemade wills include:

- The will being incorrectly signed and witnessed.
- Including assets or giving away assets that technically don't form part of their estate, such as jointly owned property or superannuation, or company assets such as vehicles owned by the company rather than their shares in the company.
- Unclear wording that results in misunderstandings of what was intended.
- Failing to appoint an executor (legal figurehead for the estate).

Rectifying any of these problems will require someone to apply to the Supreme Court for the court to interpret the will, which can be costly. Ultimately, the will can be declared invalid, and this can lead to assets being distributed in accordance with the intestacy provisions I mentioned.

CONTESTING A WILL

Claims made against the estate are made when family members feel that they haven't been left enough under the will. Even an unsuccessful claim can be quite costly to defend and can be damaging to the family. There are often pragmatic settlements reached where someone is paid some funds, even if the executor of the family feels that the application is unwarranted, simply to avoid legal costs in defending the claim.

Unfortunately, there is no way to stop an eligible person from making a claim, but there are steps that one can take to minimise or prevent a claim from being made. Getting some proper legal advice is the first port of call, as well as making sure that you can provide adequately for your family.

COMPLEX FAMILIES

Mixed families present certain challenges with respect to estate planning, and they need special consideration. You'll need to consider how to balance the needs of your children from your first relationship and the needs of your current spouse and children with that spouse. You should seek legal advice from a lawyer with respect to how best to address the various needs of your family members. Again, there are certain strategies that can be employed to try to avoid the risk of a claim.

TESTAMENTARY TRUST

A testamentary trust is a special trust formed under the direction of your will and is only established in the event of your death. Upon your passing, the assets in your will are transferred to a trust and managed by a trustee on behalf of the intended beneficiaries.

The main benefit of a testamentary trust is that it provides a greater control over the assets. For example, if your children are young or you are concerned about a beneficiary's ability to manage money, the trust can be structured to limit the amount of money distributed. The other benefit of a testamentary trust is that it can provide some taxation relief to the beneficiaries, regardless of age.

REVIEWING YOUR WILL

There are several automatic triggers that should prompt you to update your estate plan:

- Marriage will revoke a will, except where the will is made in contemplation of marriage.
- Divorce will invalidate any appointment or gifts to your previous spouse.

There are many other events that won't have any automatic changes, but should trigger a visit to the solicitor make a new will.

For example, if you've started a new relationship or if you've separated from a partner, there won't be any automatic effects upon your estate plans, but no doubt you would not wish for your ex-spouse to receive your estate upon your death, and you may have provided for that in your last will.

If you've had more children or grandchildren or you welcome stepchildren into the family, or if anyone named in the will has passed on, changes will likely need to be made. If there has been a disability of a family member that might require you to make certain provisions for them under your estate plan, you should take that into account. A family member might be experiencing separation, so you might want to take steps to ensure that their inheritance doesn't form part of their matrimonial pool in the event of a family law property settlement or orders.

SUPERANNUATION AND BINDING DEATH NOMINATIONS

In this day and age, many of us are holding a significant portion of our wealth in our superannuation. What most people don't appreciate, however, is that your superannuation does not automatically form part of your estate. If you don't provide specific instructions, your superannuation trustee will decide who gets your death benefit. This exposes many estates to the risk that the intended distribution may become skewed.

Similarly, you'll want to ensure that super stays out of your estate, so it doesn't become vulnerable to any will challenge that may be made against your estate after your death.

LIFE INSURANCE

Life insurance – much like super – is also an asset that doesn't necessarily form part of your estate. It will depend on who owns your life insurance policy and who the beneficiary is under your policy.

OTHER IMPORTANT DOCUMENTS

Other documents that form part of the estate plan include an enduring power of attorney and your appointment of a medical treatment decision-maker. It's important to recognise that these documents relate to circumstances that will arise or that may arise during your lifetime. So, whereas a will would only come into effect after you've passed away, an enduring power of attorney or an appointment of medical treatment decision-maker provides for certain people to make decisions in respect to your affairs whilst you're alive, but when you no longer have the capacity to make those decisions yourself.

If you don't have these documents prepared, there can be a lot of administrative work required to put yourself in the same position that you would be in if you had made the documents. If you don't make the documents, someone will have to apply to be your administrator and/or guardian. The courts have the power to appoint anyone who applies, but they may also consider that person not to be a suitable choice.

In summary, no one wants to think about death and illness, but it is incredibly important to make plans. It's essential not only to preserve the wealth of your family, but also to preserve the family itself. Not having these documents in place often leads to many headaches for your loved ones, and at a time when they are already dealing with a lot of grief in respect to your loss of capacity or your death.

ESTATE PLANNING AUDIT

An estate planning audit includes both a review of your current estate planning needs and your current financial situation.

Completing this once a year gives you the confidence that your current plan both reflects your current situation and personal wishes, as well as ensuring it is up to date with current laws and legislation. By doing so, you ensure your own peace of mind and protect your loved ones by minimising the risks of conflicts and legal issues, as well as minimising tax implications with changing legislation.

By answering the questions in the estate plan audit in the workbook, you will obtain an overview of your own requirements and identify areas that you need to either update or implement, to ensure they align with your wishes and personal goals. Some of these amendments can include making changes to beneficiaries or other legal representatives, and updating specific assets.

 Fill out your estate plan audit provided in the workbook.

ESTATE PLANNING GOALS

An estate plan involves making crucial decisions about how your assets will be distributed upon your death. Understanding your personal goals is an essential step in creating an estate plan that accurately reflects your wishes and intent to provide for your loved ones. It allows for a plan to be specific to your own needs and preferences.

When creating an estate plan, there are several considerations that need to be taken into account. Some of the questions you should ask yourself include:

- Who do you want to inherit your assets?
- Do you intend to gift any assets to charity?
- Who do you feel is the most appropriate person to oversee your estate?
- Are you confident they understand and will follow your wishes?

- Do you have minor children who will need to be cared for?
- Who will you name as a guardian to your children?
- How will your estate be divided amongst your beneficiaries? (Equally? Specific amounts or percentages?)
- Do you want to restrict any access to funds for any beneficiaries (eg. until children reach a certain age)?
- Do you have any special circumstances that need to be considered (eg. blended family, business or trust entities)?
- Do you have any specific wishes for end-of-life treatments, organ donations and funeral arrangements?
- Have you nominated a beneficiary of your superannuation?
- Do you foresee any disputes arising from your wishes?

Please remember this list of questions is a guide only.

Head to the workbook to fill out your own estate plan goals.

REFLECTIONS AND LESSONS

① > ② > ③ > ④ > ⑤

Remember   Understand   Analyse   Apply   Extend

1. REMEMBER:

What were some of the specific skills, knowledge, or habits that you gained during this chapter?

2. UNDERSTAND:

Why are these accomplishments important for your financial fitness? How will they impact your life in the short-term and long-term?

3. ANALYSE:

What were some of the positive/helpful behaviours you've noticed you have? And what were some of the negative/unhelpful behaviours that you need to be aware of going forward?

REFLECTIONS & ACTIONS
4. APPLY:

Where and how can you apply the knowledge and skills you gained during this chapter? What are some of the specific areas where you can apply your new financial literacy, and how will you do so?

5. EXTEND:

How can you use the knowledge and skills you gained during this chapter in other parts of your life? How can you extend the benefits of financial fitness beyond just your personal finances?

Just as rest and recovery are critical components of physical fitness, reflection plays a vital role in becoming financially fit.

It allows us to pause, take a step back, and evaluate our progress towards our goals.

Without reflection, we risk falling into old habits and repeating the same mistakes.

By reflecting on our actions and decisions, we can gain insight into what works for us and what doesn't, and make the necessary adjustments to achieve success.

So just as we make time for stretching and warm-ups in our physical fitness routine, we must also prioritise regular reflection to keep our minds and actions aligned with our goals.

"We cannot change what we are not aware of, and once we are aware, we cannot help but change."

Sheryl Sandberg

CHAPTER 11

MONEY MASTERY

Achieving Financial Fitness at
All Levels of Your Life

Congratulations! You have reached the final chapter of the book. You've worked through a lot of content so far to get to this point. You have developed a solid understanding of the mindset and essential skills required to master your money and create a path to financial freedom. The focus now is on making the final decisions and taking action!

It is time to take responsibility for your current financial situation, but more importantly, own your decisions on where to next, using your growth mindset.

> *No matter where you are in your financial journey*
> *– don't quit. Don't give up. It's never too late.*

It is not enough to write down goals and plans. It is time to be proactive and take continuous action towards achieving them, and of course celebrating the achievements.

This chapter is the time for you to really implement the lessons you've learnt.

DECISIONS

Now that you have finished the book, there are critical decisions you need to make to put what you have learnt into practice. This is where creating habits is the key to your financial success.

Although most people go into the new year with the best intentions to maintain their resolutions, it doesn't take long to give up on goals or even forget them entirely. When you shift from making a once-a-year change to creating lasting change, you will achieve more than you probably believe is possible.

> *I know I am trying to force myself to do something when I use words like "should", "have to" and "must" – but when I change my mindset to "can", I achieve so much more.*

Resolving to do something differently in the future is usually driven by something we are unhappy with, or when we are feeling unfulfilled. Resolutions continue to connect us to the negativity. Transforming your life requires deep self-reflection, overcoming your limiting beliefs and building new habits. The best New Year's resolutions are about setting goals and making a dedicated plan to achieve them.

You might be surprised, but I'm about to put investments and fitness together. A starvation diet doesn't work – and it's the same with financials. Whatever you decide to do in terms of investing, it must be sustainable. I'm a big believer in small, consistent habits over time. If you keep doing these little things while you grow, you will get those long-term results. It's the same with diets – diets don't work, but building up consistent healthy habits will help you achieve your goals.

Educating yourself is key – learn different techniques, learn what's out there, find what suits you and feels comfortable for you. Make sure it doesn't keep you up at night. Set specific, measurable and achievable goals. This means that you have to go back to what your visions and dreams are, and start to create some goals around them. Treat yourself occasionally – regular indulgences are okay. We do not need to be so stringent with our spending habits, because we can enjoy life and the rewards that come from working so hard.

CREATING GOOD MONEY HABITS

Creating good money habits can allow you to live more comfortably and stress less about your financial future. A change in your financial situation starts with a change in how you think about money.

Many of us make it a goal to finally get our finances in shape. Becoming physically fit and financially fit are quite similar when it comes to achieving the goals. So, here's how I recommend that you approach creating your money habits:

1. Set specific goals. Like all goal setting, financial fitness needs to be both measurable and attainable.
2. The hardest part is starting. There will always be competing priorities. Think of it as taking one step at a time.
3. A starvation diet doesn't work. What you choose to do must be sustainable. There is no quick fix. Waiting for a bonus or a tax return will not develop healthy habits. Small actions multiply over time.
4. Educating yourself is key. Identify the gaps in your knowledge and then aim to gain as much knowledge as possible with what is available to you.

5. Try different techniques. Choose what feels more comfortable and less stressful, as you are more likely to continue with this.

6. Develop small consistent habits. Small habits practised over time build long-term success.

7. Treat yourself occasionally. Irregular indulgences keep us happy and make sure we're enjoying the benefits of our hard work.

Your financial success will come down to your financial habits. Each financial decision you make will reinforce the habit, both good and bad.

As Steve Jobs famously said, "Focusing is about saying no." This attitude can be transferred to your money mindset. Every time you consider spending money, ask yourself, "Is this aligned with my long-term goals?" and "Will something suffer if I do this?"

Here are two final tips when starting out on your money journey.

1. Spend mindfully. Remember, you don't need to spend more as you earn more. Spending more is not going to help you to reach your goals. The more money you spend now, the longer it will take for you to reach your goals.

2. Don't go broke trying to look rich. Money talks and wealth whispers. Focus your energy on building your wealth instead of spending it. Don't compare yourself to friends or family. Stick to your own goals.

Creating good money habits will require you to do more than set up your financial goals. Setting and implementing habits that are achievable to stick to will play a much more significant role in creating financial success.

MORE/LESS EXERCISE

This exercise will help you figure out what is working for you and what isn't, and explore what you can do to change this, work towards your goals and prioritise the habits you would like to create.

- Revisit your financial goals that you set in chapter 2. Break these into your timeframes – short-term, medium-term and long-term.
- Identify what is currently working for you. Look at the financial decisions and actions you currently have in place that are having a positive impact on you achieving your goals. For example, you may already be salary sacrificing money into superannuation.
- Identify what is not working. Similarly, acknowledge the specifics in your current situation that are counterproductive to you achieving these goals. An example may be only paying the minimum on your credit card, even though you have available funds to pay more.
- Determine what you need more of to continue your path to successfully achieving your goals in your set timeframe. Look at the financial decisions and actions you are taking that you have the capacity to do more of. For example, this

might be increasing the amount of funds you are directing to your regular investment plan.

- Determine what you could benefit from doing less of. The most common standout here will be cutting down on your discretional spending across one or more expense categories that could assist in freeing up money to put towards your financial goals. *An example of this is cutting down spending on entertainment.*

You can do the More/Less exercise in the workbook.

ACTIONS

To help you work out what important tasks you might still need to complete, I've come up with this checklist for you.

YOUR ACTION LIST

- ☐ Update your contact details with any providers.
- ☐ Confirm your tax file number has been provided to superannuation and for investments.
- ☐ Confirm you know the balances of your investments (including superannuation).
- ☐ Confirm you have a valid beneficiary (or beneficiaries) nominated on your superannuation.
- ☐ Make sure you are comfortable with the levels of personal insurance cover.
- ☐ Review the interest rate on your home loan.
- ☐ Commit to repaying your credit card in full by .... (date).
- ☐ Commit to paying an extra $............................ into your home loan on a .... (time) basis.
- ☐ Commit to contributing $............................ into your super on a .... (time) basis.
- ☐ Check your notice of intent to claim for superannuation.
- ☐ Commit to contributing $............................ into an investment option on a .... (time) basis.
- ☐ Ensure you have a will and power of attorney.
- ☐ If not, commit to completing this by .... (date).
- ☐ Ensure you have put a review date of 6 and 12 months into your diary to repeat this process.

CELEBRATIONS

So now you get to celebrate your wins, your achievements and you!

> *You've done hard things already – it's time to celebrate these wins and make a list of what you've achieved. This includes things you are proud of and things that make you remarkable.*

Celebrating is a hard one for me, but something I have done from day dot of being an employee is put some of the money I make aside. Whatever I got as a tax return, I put some aside as an investment, and it was a reward for me to get my money working for me. I also buy something purely for myself. I still do that when I overreach targets. These are my ways of celebrating myself and my wins.

As I get older, or I guess busier as we all do when we're working, probably my greatest reward is taking my daughters out for dinner and us all celebrating together. It's important to me to lead by example with my girls and celebrate with them to let them know that I finished my first course or that my hard work has resulted in me leading a workshop at a company. For me, the reward is seeing them understand that I really work hard to provide for our family.

Think about how you want to reward yourself and celebrate your achievements, and then set some goals to get there. Consider how to celebrate both big and small wins, then put these specific rewards and goals into your financial goal sheet as well.

> *We often just push on through and don't celebrate the things that we have done. What wins do you want to celebrate and how are you going to celebrate them?*

REFLECTIONS AND LESSONS

Now that you've taken some time to reflect on how far you have come and how you celebrate yourself and your achievements, it's time to give yourself some feedback about your progress. Don't forget that everything you've learnt throughout this will only be useful and fruitful for you if you put it into action, continuously review it, and make yourself accountable for it.

Please take some time to answer the questions below.

Questions to think about:

What is your biggest takeaway from the book?

What is one thing you plan to do differently when you finish reading this book?

Do you feel Financially Fit?

....

....

....

....

"All our dreams
can come true,
if we have the
courage to
pursue them."

Walt Disney

CONCLUSION

Achieving increased financial independence involves understanding your financial situation and having the resources to create a solid financial foundation that provides stability for both you and your family. This freedom allows you to make financial decisions that align with your personal and financial goals.

Throughout this book, my intention has been to serve as your guide, providing you with knowledge and tools to make informed decisions about your finances. My goal is for you to feel empowered and confident, so you can avoid financial missteps that may negatively impact your future.

By recognising your personal and financial value, you are already on the path to improving your financial wellbeing. The benefits of building your financial fitness are numerous, including a significant step towards achieving gender equality and financial empowerment for women.

Now, it's your turn to keep the conversation going. Talk to your family, friends, and daughters about the importance of financial confidence. Together, we can work towards closing the gender gap in the financial realm.

Thank you for investing your time in reading this book.

xx *Amanda*

MY TOP FIVE
FINANCIALLY
FIT TIPS

Business Edition

Over the years I've been in business, I've made plenty of mistakes, and learnt lots along the way, so I wanted to share my five biggest tips for being financially fit.

This chapter is all about tips, tricks, external help and things to think about.

Firstly, here are my five tips for being in business, and what I've learnt the most about from being in business and advising businesses for the last 20-odd years.

OVERVIEW

1. You don't know, and can't know, everything – ask for help.
2. Your team should all work together for your success – you don't need to decide between an accountant and a financial advisor. There's room for both.
3. Money talks and wealth whispers.
4. Learn about, and consider the benefits of, a family trust.
5. Pay yourself!

Tip 1: Ask for help

> *Ask for help and surround yourself with people who want to see you succeed on your journey.*

Firstly, you have to ask for help when you need it. We don't know everything; my knowledge has come from life experience, being on the path with businesses and sharing their triumphs and tragedies, and being able to look at that and learn as we go through it. It takes a village to run a business, so ask for help and surround yourself with people who want to see you succeed on your journey.

I have several colleagues and my accountant, who will always pick up the phone and talk me through anything I need help with, whether that's for myself or for my client. My lawyer is always open to me saying, "What do you think about this?" What I'm really trying to emphasise is asking for help where your pain points are. Knowing your pain points means that you can identify areas that you struggle with the most, and then find the right person to teach you or help handle specific tasks for you.

For me, my pain point is marketing and social media. I feel awkward putting myself out there and speaking about myself. So, I outsource that area of my business.

I recently hired a business coach to help me dive deeper into an area of my business that I am getting immense satisfaction from, my online course that teaches women how to become financially fit. During my Financially Fit Women course, I realised I was loving delivering the course so much that I needed to delve further into that field, so I hired this business coach for myself, not so much to scale up the course but to see where I want to take it and what I want to do.

I'm lucky I understand finances, so I don't need any help in that area, but for many women, this is the area that intimidates them the most. So, to those people, I would say that financial advisors and accountants are your friends.

Don't think that you need to know everything and don't pressure yourself.

Tip 2: 'Accountants vs financial advisors' is a fallacy

> *The idea of 'accountants versus financial advisors' is a fallacy. It shouldn't be that way – there is always room for both.*

When I speak to people about financial planning, the biggest objection I hear is, "But I have an accountant." My response to that is, first and foremost, that we are both working for the client – so therefore, we should be able to communicate effectively and offer you our combined knowledge.

If I don't have a relationship with a client's accountant, I ask the client to send me their financials before lodgement. This way, I can get a feel for what their accountant is planning for that particular year.

I had a client, and like I do with every client, I asked him to send me his financials before launch. I didn't have a relationship with his accountant, so I asked my client to send me his financials before the end of the financial year so that I could get a feel for what the accountant was planning in that particular year. One year, my client was about to sell a business and we did all of this strategy work. He sent me his accounts because the accountant was a grumpy old man who didn't think that a young female financial advisor would have any value.

While I was looking through these accounts, I essentially found that there was $350,000 in tax that I could save my client, and the accountant hadn't been open to me, so we hadn't been able to work on this together. I had an open chat with my client and he went to the accountant to sit down and go through it all, and I saved the client the $350,000, which was a great feeling because I really delivered for the client.

In my experience, accountants are quite reactive in nature; we give accountants our facts and figures at the end of the financial year, so they're working with historic figures. Often as business owners, we will send our financials across late because we're so busy, especially if we're wanting to watch our financials until the last minute. Sometimes you're giving your accountant months to make changes, so it's very reactive. This means that they are working with historical data all of the time. We often give them the data a little bit later because we're business owners and we're so busy, and often the last thing we do is have our accounts ready. We might delay as long as possible to keep the money in our own bank, so sometimes we're giving our accountant half a year to make any changes.

Financial advisors, on the other hand, are proactive – we plan ahead. Financial advisors should be talking to each other, talking to the accountant, talking to the business owners. We plan ahead, setting financial goals for the future and planning for how you can reach these goals.

If you have an accountant and you're not ready to engage a financial advisor or someone else to help you with the business and financial planning process yet, I suggest you watch your accounts and business so that you can actually see the results and plan for the year. Lodge your returns early so that you can see the result and plan for the year ahead accordingly.

Tip 3: Money talks and wealth whispers

To illustrate this tip, I'm going to tell you a story about a wonderful client of mine. This particular woman moved to England, and started a very famous online clothing store. I didn't know her then, but when she moved back to Australia, she had unfortunately divorced her husband and got paid out of the business. This payout was around $6 million, of which she used the majority to buy a home in South Yarra in Melbourne, and then a couple hundred thousand was invested in some startup companies that her friends and accountants suggested.

She used her money to talk instead of her wealth to whisper – she had the fancy Range Rover and the $6 million house. She bought her house outright, but the Range Rover was financed to the max and her cost of living was huge.

She came back to Australia without a regular paying job; she sits on the board of a couple of companies and did a bit of consulting work, but she couldn't fund her lifestyle without a regularly paid job, so she was living outside her means.

We started working together to help her be more financially fit, and I remember her calling me one day to tell me about how our work had helped her. She told me that she had gone to the shops to buy a new dress for an art gallery opening, but my voice was ringing in her head saying, "Don't buy a new dress," so she wore a dress she had worn before.

There had been two issues with her initial approach: she couldn't keep up with her lifestyle because she didn't seek advice to start with, and she didn't know what to do with her money. She hadn't come to me prior to making these financial decisions – if she had, I would have suggested a less expensive house and more profitable investments. The issue with buying a $6 million house in the suburb she loved was that it wasn't increasing at all. This meant every single cent went into an asset that wasn't making any money.

> *Money talks and wealth whispers – work hard to build the life that you want financially in the long-term, not just to deliver every day. To become wealthy, you have to invest wisely and set yourself up for long-term prosperity.*

Yes, sacrifices may need to be made, but when I work with clients on their financial plans, I keep their priorities, values and aspirations in mind to find a balance between living their best life now and later.

Tip 4: Family trusts

> *Family trusts give business owners flexibility and protection in life as we get to distribute funds as we see fit and as our children get older.*

With family trusts, you don't have to distribute down; you can also distribute up to family members.

Like everything, there's a fine line between the cost of starting a family trust and the value it adds in the long-term. My family trust is where I do all my investing, as I can utilise the tax brackets of income coming down to my girls once they're allowed, and so that I can protect my assets from getting into other people's hands. As it sounds, family trusts keep family money.

This is a very quick tip, but I want you to consider family trusts, understand them, and always keep them in the back of your mind. Once your business starts to grow, you should speak to your financial advisor or accountant about setting up a family trust.

Tip 5: Pay yourself

> *My fifth and most important tip is to pay yourself. If you are not already paying yourself, I want you to start today.*

I want a regular amount of money coming out of your business account and into your personal account.

If you are paying yourself, then give yourself a slight increase. Why? Because, by reading this book, you are upskilling yourself. Think of it like this: if you were working for someone else and learnt a new skill, you would get a pay rise. So, if you are paying yourself, I want you to celebrate the fact that you are learning and all the knowledge you're gaining, and I want you to give yourself a pay rise.

FINANCIAL TERMINOLOGY GLOSSARY

GENERAL FINANCIAL TERMS GLOSSARY

Accounts payable:

Refers to any outstanding debts or obligations a business owes to vendors and suppliers for the purchase of goods and services not yet paid for. Accounts payable is recorded as a current liability on the balance sheet, meaning it will typically be repaid within the financial year.

Accounts receivable:

Refers to money owed to the business by customers or clients for goods or services that have been sold, but not yet paid for. It is recorded as a current asset on the balance sheet, and typically will be repaid within the financial year.

Assets:
Refers to a resource that is owned or controlled by a business and has the potential to produce economic value in the future or reduce expenses. Examples include cash, property, vehicles and equipment.

Balance sheet:
Refers to a financial statement of the business that shows the business's overall position at a given point in time. It provides a snapshot of the business's assets, liabilities and equity, the total of which is used to calculate the business's net worth.

Break-even point:
Refers to the point at which a business generates enough profit to cover its expenses.

Budget:
Refers to a financial plan that demonstrates the expected income and expenses of a business and is typically broken down by month, quarter and year. The purpose of a budget is to ensure expenses are not going to exceed projected income and resources are being allocated effectively.

Capital:
Refers to the financial resources of a business that are available for investment in assets or to finance operations. There is debt and equity capital. Capital is an essential resource for companies to finance operations but also to generate income or grow wealth.

Cashflow:
Refers to the difference between cash inflows, in the form of receipts, and cash outflows, in the form of payments made usually tracked during a specific time period, being a week, month or year.

Chart of accounts:
Refers to a comprehensive list of all of the accounts used by a business to record financial transactions. It will include income and expense accounts as well as liability, asset and equity accounts.

Company (limited liability):
Refers to a company in which the rights of shareholders are limited by the amount of capital, or number of shares, they have invested in the company. The benefit of limited liability is that the personal assets of shareholders are not at risk should the company become insolvent or face legal action.

Depreciation:
Refers to the reduction in the value of an asset over time due to general wear and tear and obsolescence. Depreciation is calculated by dividing the cost of the asset by its estimated useful life and recording a portion of the cost as an expense in each financial year.

Drawings:
Refers to the funds that an owner or partner of a business withdraws from the business for their personal use. They represent a reduction in the owner's equity within the business.

Gross profit (also known as net sales):
Refers to the profit a business generates after deducting direct costs from total revenue. It is often referred to as net sales.

GST:
Refers to the Goods and Services Tax (GST) which is a tax of 10% on most goods, services and other items sold or consumed within Australia.

Margin:
Refers to the difference between the revenue generated by a business's sales and the costs associated with producing and selling the business's product or service. Margin is often spoken about in terms of a percentage, showing the proportion of profit generated for each dollar of sales.

Net assets:
Refers to the total assets of a business, less its total liabilities. It is often defined as the residual value of a business's assets after all debts and other obligations have been paid.

Net profit (also known as your bottom line):
Refers to the amount of profit that a business has made after deducting all of its expenses from total gross profit. It represents

the earnings that are available to be distributed to owners or shareholders or retained within the business.

Partnership:
Refers to a business structure within Australian in which two or more people carry on a business with the view of generating a profit. It is not a separate legal entity from the individual partners, meaning they will be personally liable for all debts and obligations of the partnership.

Profit:
Refers to the amount of money a business has made after deducting all of its expenses from its total revenue.

Profit and loss statement (also known as an income statement):
Refers to a financial statement of the business that summarises the revenues, costs and expenses over a specified period, typically a month, a quarter or a year. The difference between the revenue and the expenses displayed in the business's profit and loss statement is the business's net income or loss for the period.

Return on investment (ROI):
Refers to a financial metric used to measure how efficient a business is at generating profit from the original equity provided by its owners or shareholders. It is a useful tool for assessing the return you are generating on the money you have invested and helps investors evaluate the profitability of

their investment. To calculate ROI, you divide net profit by the cost of the investment and multiply by 100 to generate a percentage.

Revenue (also known as turnover):
Refers to the total amount of money earned by a business from its normal trading activities, such as the selling of goods or services, before deducting expenses.

SMSF:
Refers to a self-managed superannuation fund. It is a type of fund in Australia that is managed by the member themselves, rather than by a professional fund manager or trustee. They are still regulated by the ATO, which means that the member is responsible for ensuring the super fund complies with the relevant superannuation and tax laws.

Sole trader:
Refers to a business structure in which an individual carries on a business on their own and will be personally liable for all debts and obligations of the entity. As a sole trader, the individual maintains complete control over the business and is entitled to all profits, however they are also responsible for meeting all reporting and financial obligations.

Superannuation:
Refers to a retirement savings scheme within Australia. It is designed to help individuals save and plan for retirement by providing investment options for a portion of their income over

the course of their working life. The money deducted from an individual's pay for superannuation must be sent to a complying fund.

Tax invoice:
Refers to a document issued by a supplier of goods or services to their customers that is required to contain certain information about the transaction by law. In many countries, including Australia, a valid tax invoice is a requirement for being able to claim GST or tax credits, as well as deductions for expenses purchased within the company.

Trust:
Refers to a legal structure in which a trustee holds and manages property or assets on behalf of one or more beneficiaries. The trustee must manage the assets of the trust in accordance with the trust deed and the wishes of beneficiaries. There are several types of trusts in Australia, including a discretionary trust, unit trust, testamentary trust and a hybrid trust.

Working capital:
Refers to the funds a business has available to cover its day-to-day operations and to meet short-term financial obligations. It is the difference between the current assets and current liabilities of the business.

INSURANCE GLOSSARY

Beneficiary:

Refers to the person or entity designated to receive the benefits of a policy or contract upon the death of the insured, or on the occurrence of the insured event, such as a disability or critical illness.

Benefit period:

Refers to the length of time during which benefits will be payable under an insurance policy for a covered event, such as an illness or injury.

Claim:

Refers to a formal request made by an insured person or entity to an insurance company to seek coverage or reimbursement for a covered loss or damage. Claims are typically subject to investigation and evaluation by the insurance company.

Cover:

Refers to the scope and extent of protection provided by an insurance policy. Coverage specifies the risks, events or damages that are covered by the policy, as well as the limits, conditions and exclusions of the coverage.

Exclusion:

Refers to specific risks, events or damages that are not covered by an insurance policy. Exclusions are usually listed in the insurance policy and may vary depending on the type of coverage and the specific policy.

Indemnity policy:
Refers to a type of policy that reimburses the policyholder for the financial loss suffered under a covered event, up to specified policy limits. An indemnity policy is designed to restore the insured policyholder to the same financial position they were in prior to the occurrence of the covered loss.

Insured:
Refers to the individual or entity that is covered by an insurance policy and is entitled to receive benefits in the event of a covered loss or claim. The insured may or may not be the same as the policyholder.

Insurer:
Refers to the company or organisation that provides insurance coverage in exchange for the payment of a premium. The insurer assumes the risk of the potential loss or liability of the covered event, up to the policy limit.

Level premium:
Refers to a premium payment structure where the policyholder pays the same premium amount for the duration of the policy term. The premium amount does not change even as the policyholder ages or the risk of insuring the policyholder increases.

Loading:
Refers to an additional charge or fee added to the base premium of an insurance policy to reflect an increased level of risk associated

with the policyholder. It is normally expressed as a percentage of the base premium and there are a number of factors which may determine the amount of the loading.

Lump sum:
Refers to a one-off payment made to the policyholder or the beneficiary upon the occurrence of a covered event, eg. death, disability or critical illness.

Monthly benefit:
Refers to a regular payment made to the policyholder or beneficiary each month in the occurrence of a covered event, eg. death, disability or critical illness.

Policyholder:
Refers to the individual or entity that owns an insurance policy and is entitled to the benefits from the protection provided by the policy. The policyholder is responsible for paying the premiums and complying with the terms and conditions of the insurance policy.

Policy term:
Refers to the period for which an insurance policy provides coverage. Policy terms are usually specified in the insurance policy and may be renewed or terminated at the end of the term.

Premium:
Refers to the amount of money an individual or entity pays to an insurance company for an insurance policy. It is usually

paid monthly or annually and is the cost of obtaining insurance coverage.

Stepped premium:
Refers to a premium payment structure in which the premium amount increases over time as the policyholder ages or the risk of insuring them increases.

Underwriting:
Refers to the process by which an insurance company assesses the risk of insuring an individual or entity and determines the terms, conditions and premiums for an insurance policy. Underwriting involves assessing various factors, including age, health, occupation and claims history, to determine the risk profile of the insured.

Waiting period:
Refers to a specific period that must pass before the coverage under an insurance policy becomes effective. The policyholder will not be eligible to receive benefits or coverage for certain types of events such as illness or injury during this period.

INVESTMENT GLOSSARY

Active investment:

Refers to an investment strategy where an investor actively makes buying and selling decisions with the goal of outperforming the market or a specific benchmark. The investor will need to rely on their own research, analysis and predictions to identify which investments they believe will generate above average returns. This strategy is designed to take advantage of short-term market opportunities and is therefore a riskier strategy than passive investment.

Asset class:

Refers to a group or category of financial investments that have similar characteristics and behave in a similar way, ie. similar risk-return profiles and historical performance patterns. Asset classes may include shares, bonds, cash and cash equivalents or even real estate.

Capital:

Refers to the financial resources or funds that are available for investing in various assets. Capital can come from personal savings, investment accounts, superannuation accounts, inheritance or other forms of financing.

Diversification:

Refers to spreading investment funds across a range of assets to minimise risk and maximise potential returns. The aim is to reduce the impact of any fluctuations in the performance of one asset class on the portfolio as a whole by investing in a number of different asset classes.

Dividends:
Refers to payments made by a corporation or company to its shareholders as a distribution of profits or earnings. When a company generates profits, it may choose to retain profits within the company or reinvest in its operations or to pay out a portion of those profits to shareholders in the form of dividends.

Expense ratio:
Refers to the annual fee charged by an index fund or exchange-traded fund to cover the costs of managing and operating the fund. It is expressed as a percentage of the fund's total assets under management.

Growth:
Refers to an investment strategy focused on achieving above-average growth in value over time. It is typically characterised by more risky investments that have a greater potential for capital appreciation but also tend to be more volatile. Growth strategies tend to be favoured by investors who have a longer-term investment horizon and do not require an immediate or predictable return.

Income:
Refers to an investment strategy focused on generating regular and consistent income streams in the form of dividends, interest or even rental repayments. These investment strategies

are often favoured by investors who are seeking a regular source of income to meet their needs such as retirement or living expenses.

Index:
Refers to a benchmark or a measure of the performance of a group of investments. An index is usually designed to track the performance of a specific market, sector or asset class and is then used as a reference to measure the performance of investments relative to the overall market.

Liquidity:
Refers to the ease and speed with which an investment can be bought and sold in the market without significantly impacting the price. It is ultimately the ability to convert an investment into cash quickly and with limited costs.

Passive investment:
Refers to an investment strategy where an investor seeks to generate returns by tracking a benchmark or market index, rather than actively seeking to outperform the market. The goal is to match the performance of the benchmark or index, through investment in low-cost index funds or exchange-traded funds. These funds hold a diversified portfolio of securities that represent the underlying index, providing a lower risk exposure for investors to a larger range of investment options.

Portfolio:

Refers to a collection of investment assets owned by an individual, organisation or entity. A portfolio should typically include a diverse range of investments in order to spread the risk across the portfolio and maximise returns.

Volatility:

Refers to the degree of fluctuation in the price or value of an investment over time. Volatility is often used as a measure of risk; more volatile investments are generally considered to be riskier.

SUPERANNUATION GLOSSARY
General terms
Accumulation fund:
The most common type of super fund. Retirement benefits are calculated based on contributions received plus investment returns less fees and taxes.

Accumulation phase:
A period when you are contributing to your account. All contributions made during this phase are locked away (preserved) until your retirement.

Age pension:
Fortnightly government payments for eligible people who have reached the age pension age, meet the residency requirements, and pass the assets and income means tests.

Age pension age:
Age at which you become eligible to receive a regular age pension payment. The age varies depending on your date of birth. Currently 66 years and 6 months, but will progressively increase to age 67 by 1 July 2023.

Asset allocation:
Your mix or allocation of investment assets across different asset classes. Asset allocations can be customised to suit your investment goals and risk profile.

Beneficiary:
A person or a number of people who receive money, or something beneficial, from another individual, group or organisation. In the event of your death, your super fund is required to pay your super balance and the proceeds of any insurance cover to your beneficiaries, or if there are no eligible beneficiaries, to any person who has a fair claim. It is therefore important you nominate one or more beneficiaries. A beneficiary can be your spouse or partner, or someone who is dependent on you (financially or otherwise), or your estate or legal personal representative. You can make a binding nomination, preferred nomination or reversionary nomination.

Binding death benefit nomination (BDBN):
With a valid BDBN, super fund trustees must pay your super death benefit to the nominated beneficiaries, in the proportions you list. BDBNs override the normal trustee discretion on paying a super death benefit.

Condition of release:
Condition you must meet to legally access your super benefits. Common conditions include retirement after reaching your preservation age, starting a transition-to-retirement pension and reaching age 65.

Death benefit:
When a member dies, the super fund trustee pays a death benefit (usually the member's entire account balance) to their

dependants or their estate. Usually paid as a lump sum, but can be a pension.

Inactive member account:

Super account that has not received any contributions, rollovers or transfers, or made any benefit payments within the past two years, but which has not been closed as the member is not contactable.

Member statement:

Super funds are required to provide members with a detailed statement outlining information including account transactions and balance, tax and fees paid, insurance and investment return at financial year end.

MySuper funds:

Simple, low-cost and easy-to-compare option offered by many super funds. Often the default super account for people who don't choose their own super fund when they start a new job.

Preservation age:

Minimum age at which you can withdraw your super benefits once you meet a condition of release. Different from the age at which you are eligible for the age pension.

Trustee (or trustee board/directors):

Person or group of people responsible for managing a super fund and ensuring its legal compliance on behalf of the super fund members.

Total superannuation balance (TSB):
Combined balance of your accumulation and retirement phase super savings at any point in time.

Transfer balance cap (TBC):
Introduced in July 2017, a $1.7 million cap on the amount that can be transferred to the tax-free retirement phase to start a super pension. Indexed periodically in $100,000 increments.

Transition-to-retirement (TTR or TRIS) pension:
Pension that can be started once you reach your preservation age, but before age 65. Allows you to access your super without having to stop work. Investment earnings are taxed at 15%.

Unclaimed super:
From 1 July 2019, super funds must report and pay all inactive low-balance accounts to the ATO. Includes unclaimed super of members aged 65 and over, non-member spouses and deceased members, small lost member accounts and inactive low-balance accounts.

Contributions-related terms

Contributions tax:

Tax paid on super contributions as they enter your super account. Current rates are 15% for concessional contributions, nil for non-concessional and 15% for contributions over the Division 293 threshold.

Concessional contributions:

Also known as before-tax contributions. Includes super guarantee (SG) contributions, salary sacrifice payments, award contributions and personal contributions for which you claim a tax deduction. Taxed at 15% as they enter your account.

Concessional contributions cap:

Cap limiting the amount of before-tax contributions you can make into your super account in a financial year. Contributions above the annual cap incur additional tax.

Non-concessional contributions:

Sometimes referred to as after-tax contributions, as tax has already been deducted from the money used for the contribution. The two main types are personal contributions not claimed as a tax deduction and spouse contributions.

Non-concessional contributions cap:

Maximum amount you are permitted to contribute into your super account from after-tax income within a financial year. Current annual cap is $110,000 (2021-22).

Bring-forward rule:

Rule covering non-concessional super contributions. Allows you to advance or bring forward your contributions caps from a three year period and use them over a shorter period – either all at once or as several large contributions.

Employer contribution:

Contributions made by an employer on behalf of an employee into their super account. Generally includes SG and award contributions and salary sacrifice contributions.

Superannuation guarantee (SG):

Official term for the compulsory super contributions made by your employer into your super account on your behalf. Current rate is 10.5% (2022-23) with the plan to be 12% by 2025.

Rollover:

Amount transferred between super funds, retirement savings accounts, deferred annuities or approved deposit funds.

Salary sacrifice:

Agreement between you and your employer to forego part of your future salary in return for benefits of a similar value (such as super contributions, a car or health insurance). Allows you to pay for the benefit from your before-tax salary.

Tax-deductible personal contribution:
You can claim a tax deduction for personal super contributions up to the annual concessional contributions cap ($27,500 in 2021-22) if you meet the eligibility criteria.

Carry-forward contributions:
Rule allowing you to accumulate any unused portion of your annual concessional contributions cap for up to five years. Allows you to make concessional contributions over the annual contributions cap (currently $25,000).

Co-contribution:
Contribution (up to $500) made by the Australian government into an eligible low- or middle-income earner's super account after they make a voluntary contribution.

Contribution splitting:
Rules allowing you to split your super contributions with your spouse (married or de facto) providing you meet the eligibility criteria.

Gainfully employed:
Under super law, this means doing paid work for at least 10 hours per week. Affects whether you satisfy the retirement condition of release and whether you can make super contributions after age 67.

Work test:

If you are aged 67 to 74, you must satisfy the work test to make contributions to your super fund. The test requires you to be gainfully employed for a minimum of 40 hours in any 30 consecutive day period.

Components of superannuation terms

Taxable component:

Part of a super benefit subject to tax if withdrawn before age 60. Mainly consists of concessional contributions, such as employer and salary sacrifice contributions, investment earnings and contributions claimed as a tax deduction. Further divided into taxed and untaxed elements.

Tax-free component:

Mainly the non-concessional contributions in a super account (which are from after-tax income). Can include a crystallised segment (fixed dollar figure for certain pre-July 2007 benefits).

Preserved benefits:

Super money that is 'preserved' or locked away until you reach your preservation age and meet a condition of release.

Non-preserved benefits – restricted:

Includes any employment-related contributions made before 1 July 1999, excluding employer contributions. Can't be accessed until the employment arrangement they relate to has ended.

Unrestricted non-preserved benefits:
Includes any super benefits that can be paid on demand by your super fund because you have satisfied a condition of release.

Fee-related terms

Administration fees:
Fee charged to fund members to cover expenses relating to the administration or operation of a super fund.

Advice fee:
Fee charged to cover the cost of providing financial product advice to a super fund member who requests it.

Investment fee:
Fee charged by super funds for services relating to the investment of the fund's assets. Can sometimes be referred to as an MER (management expense ratio).

Investment management performance fee:
Investment fee determined, in whole or part, by performance of an investment made by an investment manager on behalf of the super fund.

ESTATE PLANNING GLOSSARY

Beneficiary:

A person or a number of people who receive money, or something beneficial, from another individual, group or organisation. In the event of your death, your super fund is required to pay your super balance and the proceeds of any insurance cover to your beneficiaries, or if there are no eligible beneficiaries, to any person who has a fair claim. It is therefore important you nominate one or more beneficiaries. A beneficiary can be your spouse or partner, or someone who is dependent on you (financially or otherwise), or your estate or legal personal representative. You can make a binding nomination, preferred nomination or reversionary nomination.

Binding death benefit nomination (BDBN):

With a valid BDBN, super fund trustees must pay your super death benefit to the nominated beneficiaries, in the proportions you list. BDBNs override the normal trustee discretion on paying a super death benefit.

Enduring power of attorney:

Is a legal document that grants a person, referred to as the "agent", the authority to manage the estate of a deceased person. This person will be responsible for taking care of the various administrative tasks of finalising the deceased estate including selling assets, paying taxes and distributing to beneficiaries.

Executor:

An executor is a person or institution that is named in a will or appointed by a court to carry out the instructions outlined in the will after the death of the testator (the person who made the will). The executor has a fiduciary duty to act in the best interests of the estate and its beneficiaries and is responsible for managing the estate and distributing its assets according to the instructions in the will.

Intestate:

Means to die without a valid will in place specifying how the deceased person's assets and property will be distributed. Intestate succession (division of the estate) can be complex and time-consuming, and it can result in unintended consequences. Unfortunately, it may lead to assets being distributed differently to how the deceased person would have wanted, or disputes may arise among family members over the distribution of assets. To avoid these issues, it's important to have a valid will or other estate planning documents in place.

Prenup:

Also known as a prenuptial agreement, it is a legal document signed by couples prior to marriage, setting out how the couple's assets and liabilities will be divided in the event of a divorce, separation or death. Prenup agreements can cover property division and spousal support, as well as inheritance rights.

Succession plan:
The process of creating a plan to ensure a smooth transition of leadership in the event that the current leader is unable to continue fulfilling their duties, ie. retirement, incapacitation and death.

Testamentary trust:
A testamentary trust is a special trust formed under the direction of your will and is only established in the event of your death. Upon your passing, the assets in your will are transferred to a trust and managed by a trustee on behalf of the intended beneficiaries.

Will:
Also known as a last will and testament, is a legal document that outlines a person's final intentions and wishes upon their death. It provides direction regarding appointing an executor to handle their estate, distribution of assets and guardianship of children. It is an essential document in the Estate Planning process as it allows an individual to have control over their Estate even in death.

ABOUT THE AUTHOR

From the boardroom of Australia's biggest banks as a leading financial advisor to qualifying three times for the Ironman World Championships despite health issues, Amanda Thompson has never been afraid of a challenge.

As an award-winning financial advisor and founder of Endurance Financial, Amanda has, for the past two decades, specialised in offering strategic financial guidance for individuals and businesses with complex matters requiring more than textbook advice. Amanda works with a vast array of clients, each seeking personalised service and advice that goes well beyond conventional wisdom.

Recognising that each and every client has different needs, wants, dreams and goals, Amanda thrives on delivering strategic and tailored advice, drawing upon almost two decades in senior advisory roles for leading financial institutions including Westpac, Commonwealth Bank and Choice Capital.

From small to medium business owners and everyday individuals looking for financial stability, to high profile personalities and affluent families motivated to secure and protect their wealth, Amanda is dedicated to going beyond the ordinary advice and helping clients create enduring financial prosperity, designed to last for generations.

As a dynamic keynote speaker, Amanda is able to captivate audiences with her intelligent wit and real-life stories. She is particularly driven to help men and women overcome the gender biases that stand in the way of personal achievement, with lessons learnt after thriving in typically male-dominated environments.

Whether delivering financial advice or inspirational anecdotes, Amanda's philosophy is to provide unique, accountable and comprehensive information that leads to successful outcomes. Her areas of expertise in business include investment strategy, wealth creation, self-managed superannuation, personal insurance and retirement strategies. Her areas of focus in life include resilience, determination and dedication to something bigger than self.

It has always been Amanda's mantra that if you get knocked to the ground, you have to get back up again. Through her personal stories and experiences, she hopes to inspire others to find the power of resilience, determination and dedication to something bigger than self. Most of all, Amanda hopes to help others realise that love really does conquer all. Adversity is a given, but it is courage that is our choice.

CONNECT WITH US

If you would like to work with me and the team at Endurance Financial, to learn more about our Financial Mentoring or sign up for one of our courses, head to our website at www.endurancefinancial.com.au

We are also pleased to extend two special offers to all our readers.

FINANCIALLY FIT BOOTCAMP - $50 OFF USING THE CODE "FFWB2023"

Wealth is defined by so much more than the balance of your bank account.

The Financially Fit Bootcamp is an online course for those planning to achieve financial fitness. It is a practical extension of the lessons learned throughout this book.

8 specially designed modules:

Which help you dig deep into what financial success means to you and how to set goals to create it in your life.

A downloadable workbook:

Which contains all of the exercises we ask you to work through in each module and will allow you to go back and revisit your answers.

Tried-and-tested spending plans and cashflow plans:

Including how-to videos so you can feel confident creating your own personal plan.

A clear implementation plan:

For how you will become financially fit. By the end of this course, you will have a very clear understanding of how to maintain your financial fitness. We want to empower you to create a wealth protection plan for today, tomorrow, the unexpected, and the future. We walk you through mastering your money, creating good money habits, understanding your money story, and ensuring you have a great money mindset.

FINANCIALLY FIT MENTORING - $100 OFF USING THE CODE "FFWM2023"

Work with us to develop a financial blueprint and roadmap that is uniquely yours. This is because our mentoring program is like no other. It is intensive, it is surprising – it is designed to tap into your story and your personal journey, to get to the heart of your challenges – and overcome them.

We want to change the negative relationship you have with money and answer the questions you have about your future financial security. We want to ensure you no longer feel anxiety when it comes to your financial security by empowering you with the information you need to ensure success.

We approach strategy building from a unique perspective, as we believe your personal goals and financial goals are not separate entities. They are connected and they need to complement each other to achieve real positive results.

Financial Audit and Education

This package is designed to assist you to dig deep into what financial success means to you and how to set goals to create it for yourself. We provide research and review as well as up to 5 x individual sessions with Amanda. Some of the areas of Discovery and Action we include are below, however, ultimately the direction we take is driven by your specific needs.

- Your finances audit
- Goal setting

- Scaling your business
- Debt analysis and planning
- Long-term wealth creation opportunities
- Cashflow considerations
- Strategy comparisons
- Impact - putting it into action

Your personalised strategy will clearly outline what you are building towards and where to allocate money, in order to get there. It will include market analysis findings, financial projections and important milestones.

This program will give you all the tools necessary to achieve financial independence. You will leave with all the knowledge you need to take charge and handle your finances yourself. You will have a clear path forward to reach your goal – whatever that may be. You will be empowered with the knowledge you need to plan for your future.

ACKNOWLEDGEMENTS

Financially Fit Women would not have become a reality without the countless individuals within my 'village'. Whether it be advice, guidance, collaboration, or introduction, Endurance Financial and this book would be a secret without you.

To ALL of my clients: thank you for trusting me to educate and support you on your individual journeys. Your stories of overcoming obstacles and achieving personal successes are the source of inspiration for this book.

Special thanks to Carolyn and Lee for believing in my passion and this book, and especially for (continuously) giving me the polite shove I need to take a deep breath and put myself out there.

I was not expecting such an emotional rollercoaster as this book arrived at the final stages of completion. It is with deepest gratitude that I acknowledge both Kathy and Georgia – thank you both for holding my hand and working with me to create something I am truly proud of.

There are not enough words to express my love and gratitude to my mum and daughters for their unwavering support and encouragement to follow my dreams. Karyn, you have continually led by example and stood beside me and the girls. Bella and Livvy, you are my constant source of strength and inspiration. I hope you are proud of me.

I would like to thank the team at Dean Publishing, and my editors Nat and Izzy for your knowledge, insight and support throughout this journey.

Lastly, but definitely not least, thank you to all of the readers of this book. It is my hope that the pages within will help you create financial fitness and empower you to live the life of your dreams. Remember to share your story to empower the generations of strong women that will follow in your footsteps.

TESTIMONIALS

"I had the absolute pleasure of being a part of Amanda Thompson's 'Financially Fit Women' course last year, I've also had the absolute pleasure of being mentored financially by Amanda for the last three years.

I can say that it was incredibly rich in content and gave me a deeper understanding of cashflow, superannuation, salary, and more. Amanda is an absolute gem and a dream to work with! She connects with her clients on a personal level, giving tough love and inspiration just when you need it.

You'll be amazed at how much you can achieve with Amanda's guidance and expertise. I couldn't advocate Endurance Financial, Amanda and Financially Fit Women more and I wish all the people who take on this journey the very best of luck, you'll need binoculars to look back to see how far you've come. Thank you Amanda."

Fiona Luca, Founder/Director, Move with Fiona Luca

"Undertaking Amanda's Financially Fit Women online course has changed the course of our family's financial future. I've learnt so much more than I anticipated and finally feel empowered when it comes to home and business finances, accounting, forecasting, insurance, superannuation, investing and wealth creation.

Amanda's course is inclusive, welcoming and chock full of tips, tools and strategies thanks to Amanda's exceptional knowledge combined with her dedication to genuinely supporting women to understand and grow their wealth. I can't recommend her course highly enough."

Dr Jodi Richardson

"Amanda Thompson is the only person who has ever really helped me understand my finances and how to manage my business more effectively. I absolutely trust her implicitly and her advice, her guidance and her support are invaluable. There is no other woman I want to work with in the finance space. She is changing everything for me."

Jules Brooke, Founder, She's The Boss Group

"I heard Amanda speak on stage about how women can be financially fit and I was captivated. Not only did Amanda talk about money mindset in a hugely relatable way, she also gave practical and immediately actionable advice for women in business.

When it came to choosing a financial advisor to help plan my personal and business wealth-building strategy, Amanda was the first (and only!) person I wanted to speak to. Working with her has been wonderful so far. Amanda took the time to understand my financial goals, even at a micro level, and we're in the process of putting together a plan to reach them all.

I'm so excited to create this vision and plan with Amanda and highly recommend her!"

Mim Jenkinson, Digital Products Expert, Planning Pro, Podcaster + Speaker

"I have been so incredibly fortunate to witness Amanda Thompson at work and see the passion, expertise and support she provides to every one of her clients. She goes far beyond the role of a traditional financial advisor to delve into what drives and motivates her clients, and that is what really sets her apart. You will not find another financial advisor like Amanda Thompson; she is an absolute powerhouse and a true inspiration."

Georgia Graham, Founder & Director, Empowering Financial Solutions

"Amanda has been my financial advisor for the last five years. She has assisted me through some very difficult times with her caring approach combined with her excellent knowledge and passion for all she does. I love working with Amanda and her sensible practical advice."

Terri Gladwell

"For me, money has always been a scary concept to talk about. Amanda truly understands that it isn't always rainbows and roses and it's comforting to talk with someone who gets it and gets me. Having Amanda and the other women in the course has resulted in me feeling less alone in the finance world of my business."

Leah Selfe, *Collectively Assist*

ENDNOTES

1   Macquarie Dictionary 2022, *Profit,* Sydney, viewed 26 October 2022, https://www.macquariedictionary.com.au/features/word/search/?search_word_type=Dictionary&word=profit&fuzzy=on.

2   Golden Gate University Business Library 2023, *Blockchain and Cryptocurrency: Cryptocurrency*, webpage, Golden Gate University, San Francisco, viewed 26 October 2022, ggu.libguides.com/c.php?g=1157511&p=8946880.

3   Chen, J, Scott, G & Kvilhaug, S 2023, *Exchange-Traded Fund (ETF) Explanation With Pros and Cons*, webpage, Investopedia, New York, viewed 26 Octover 2022, www.investopedia.com/terms/e/etf.asp.

NUMBERS FOR CRISIS HELP AND FINANCIAL SUPPORT

Crisis Help
Lifeline: 13 11 14
24 hours a day

Beyond Blue: 1300 22 46 36
24 hours

Financial Support
National Debt Helpline: 1800 007 007
Monday to Friday, 9:30am to 4:30pm.

Mob Strong Debt Helpline: 1800 808 488.
Monday to Friday, 9:30am to 4:30pm.
For Aboriginal and Torres Strait Islander peoples.

Way Forward: 1300 045 502
Monday to Friday, 9:00am to 7:00pm

Small Business Debt Helpline
Monday to Friday. 9:00am to 5:30pm AEDT

1800 Respect: 1800 737 732
24 hours
All Financial Support Services

For more information on avenues available to seek support please visit: https://moneysmart.gov.au/managing-debt/urgent-help-with-money

www.ingramcontent.com/pod-product-compliance
Lightning Source LLC
Chambersburg PA
CBHW040847210326
41597CB00029B/4758